I0419996

Behind the Piste
An Ethnography of Women in Fencing
Joseph C Wilson

Special Thanks

"One of the greatest feelings in the world is finding a friend you never knew you had." For every friend I made along this incredible journey- from the Finnish girls who taught me how to use snapchat in Italy to the impromptu picnic chefs in Switzerland, the folks who drank out of shoes in Germany, and everyone else I met in between- this book is for you.

Prologue

"No Instructions" KATIE

When I was in high school- apart from engaging in all the angst that comes with teenage years- I took an "Early World Literature" class with Mr. Reidelberger. During the class, we learned about some of the earliest forms of storytelling from across cultures- including Old Kingdom Egypt, Ancient Judea, Pre-Classic Maya, and Aboriginal Australia. The central theme throughout cultures was four questions my teacher swore every culture around the globe asked. Where did we come from? Why are we here? Where do we go when we die? What does it all mean?

These four questions still linger in the minds of humans today and across cultures. It was of course the hero's journey throughout cultures' storytelling to answer one or more of these questions. And heroes today are still those among us we believe have answered- or at least have attempted to answer- some form of one or more of these questions. As the final test of Early World Literature class, we only needed to answer a single question. "What is a hero?"

The idea of what a hero does certainly changes with time as a culture changes- such as the idea of what it means to be a man or a woman. The idea that gender and heroism was certainly linked in various cultures four hundred years ago- but the link between heroism and gender began to break when women from Eastern Asia, the Islamic World, and Western Europe began abandoning the lives designated for them for a new life of adventure, danger, and- if lucky- fortune beyond imagining.

During the Shang and Zhou Dynasties, Chinese Emperors made offerings to their ancestors- but in a show of the masculine role over the core of the culture's faith; emperors would only pray to those ancestors of the patrilineal line- meaning they only regarded their father's ancestors as important. Even on a historical basis, the only women whose names are recorded in the historical record from these dynasties were remembered because they caused men grief in some way. (Those darn uppity women!) This could include mothers attempting to advance the careers of their sons or husbands.[1]

China's famous theme of balance with "yin and yang" came into play as well- designating separate characteristics for men and women in society and dividing acceptable place and space in China for their two genders. Women were represented by yin through the characteristics of softness, self-control, reception, passivism, reflection, and tranquility. Men were designated with yang and associated with hardness, activity, assertiveness, and domination. This helped establish a belief that these distinctions between feminine and masculine were part of a "natural order" to keep the genders separate and to keep women out of the world of men.[2]

On the other side of the continent, women gradually lost rights as nations under Islam gradually slipped from their Golden Ages of the Medieval Period. Under the Islamic faith, men and women are seen as equals- requiring the same devotions of faith, charity, and pilgrimage. In fact, the introduction of Islam to cultures during the expansion period often brought more rights to women than had previously been had in pre-Islamic counterpart cultures (such as pre-Islamic Libya for example). According to the historical record, Muhammad (the chief prophet of the faith) consulted women including Umm Waraqah whom Mohammad appointed as an imam (cleric).[3]

Towards the Seventeenth Century, women's rights in Islamic nations began to decline as gender roles began reverting back to pre-Islamic norms. Depending on the culture (which ranged from modern-day Malaysia to modern-day Portugal) included exclusion of women from education, forced veiling of women's faces or bodies, non-consensual polygyny, and sexual slavery.[4]

In Western Europe, women had lost nearly all rights held under the Roman Empire due to the patriarchal oppression of Christianity during the Medieval Period. Even during the Renaissance, women held few rights and were expected to submit themselves to their husbands. Women in Seventeenth Century England were often traded from father to husband like property, and held under social demands of piety and virtue (code for not getting uppity). Women were praised for modesty, courtesy, gentleness, affability, and silence in the presence of men.[5]

According to Renaissance European cultures, a woman's chief commodity was virginity- even to the extent that when an English explorer landed in North America and wanted to name his new colony after his queen- instead of naming it "Elizabethia" or "Elizabethland," he called it "Virginia." (Virginia is for lovers! But leave room for Jesus.) In William Shakespeare's *The Tempest*, the character Miranda is found guilty of disobedience to male authorities and expressing overt displays of emotion- stepping outside of the patriarchal structure.[6]

"Rupture" Laurie Darmon

With so many women across Eurasia held under the oppressive yoke of strict gender norms under which men could hold women- the only escape was through criminal acts. And when it came to criminal feminism- women definitely made names for themselves. In the Pacific, Indian, and Atlantic Oceans- piracy in the Age of Sail (roughly five hundred to two hundred years ago) was uncontrollable. Pirates plagued new trade routes connecting the entire globe (including Oceania, Africa, and the Americas), which increased the price for securing expensive caravans of goods. Pirates across the world easily raided trade ships, kidnapped important officials, and pillaged coastal settlements.

It was the perfect opportunity for women to cast off their oppressive patriarchal social norms- and get rich doing so. The history of pirate women goes all the way back to the Vikings who often employed women in their armies before converting to Christianity during the Medieval Period. During pre-Christian times, one Viking in particular rose through the ranks and became an early pirate queen. Lagertha (sometimes spelled Ladgerda) is rumored to have murdered her own husband after learning it was easier and more beneficial to rule without him.[7]

The traditional age of piracy or "Golden Age of Piracy" however centered around the Caribbean Sea where in the Eighteenth Century, pirates plagued trade ships and often worked as mercenary crews (privateers) during the various wars between European powers. It was here that my personal favorite pirate Anne Bonny operated. Bonny was born an illegitimate child into a middle class family in Ireland. To hide his shame, Bonny's father dressed Anne as a boy and posed as a law clerk for years. As a teen, Bonny married and moved to the Caribbean where she quickly ditched her forced marriage, joined the crew of "Calico" Jack Rackam, and became a pirate. Bonny became famous for her ability in battle, drinking contests, and dodging execution.[8]

In China, Cheng I Sao married a powerful corsair in 1801 after working as a prostitute. She then originally opened a brothel before she and her husband began building a pirate fleet to raid towns in the Western Pacific. After her husband died in 1807, Cheng inherited a fleet of hundreds of ships and tens of thousands of pirates with which she could prey on fishing vessels and supply junks in Southern China. When the combined forces of China, Portugal, and the British Empire reigned down on her; Cheng was able to escape not only unscathed, but negotiated the surrender of her fleet without battle and managed to include a clause allowing her to keep every ounce of gold she plundered throughout her career.[9]

The last queen of Morocco, Sayyida al-Hurra became a pirate when- after the death of her husband- joined forces with the Turkish pirate Barbarossa. Little is known about her pre-pirate life. Even her real name is lost to history, as Sayyida al-Hurra is simply a title (but a badass one that translates to "noble lady who is free and independent, the woman sovereign who bows to no superior authority"). While Barbarossa controlled the Eastern Mediterranean, Sayyida al-Hurra controlled the west and helped prevent outside navies from entering to combat her partner.[10]

The waterfronts of early New York City were by no means safer. One pirate known as Sadie "The Goat" haunted the city's waterfront in the 1860's, raiding boats on the Hudson and Harlem Rivers, raiding farms and mansions along the riverbanks, and kidnapping important figures for ransom.[11] Further north in Boston, Rachel Wall plagued Boston Harbor in the 1780's as a siren of the sea. When a storm passed through New England, Wall and her crew would disguise the ship as a crippled barge to lure sympathetic sailors to rescue the damsel Rachel. When they boarded, Wall's crew would kill the sailors and loot their ship.[12]

Across the Caribbean, other women took to piracy to escape oppressive patriarchies including Mary Reed (who worked with Anne Bonny) and Anne Dieu-Le-Veut. One exceptional woman (among many) was Jacquotte Delahaye also known as "Back From the Dead Red." After her mother (a Haitian) died in childbirth and her father (a Frenchman) died while she was young, "Red" was left to raise her mentally handicapped brother; and the only way to do that was by becoming a pirate. After years of success on the sea, a massive bounty was placed for her capture dead or alive. After laying low for a while to escape bounty hunters, Delahaye returned to piracy and earned her nickname.[13]

Frustrated with their societies' chosen life for them, many women across the world began taking to piracy during the Age of Sail. In Eastern Asia, the Islamic World, and Western Europe, oppressive gender norms gave adventurous women only unlawful options for engaging in their curiosity of the world. While these women certainly became criminals (and while the murderous nature of Anne Bonny and Sadie "The Goat" might not exactly be ideal role model behavior), these women helped inspire their posterity to become strong women who would make their regions of the world famous for a more "socially acceptable" outlet of sword-swinging behavior- the sport of fencing.

Chapter 1: Advance

"Conquer" AURORA

Two pirates once met on a ship en route towards a treasure hunt. The first of the two was the newly elected captain, young and new to the life of piracy in the waning Age of Sail. The other was old, seasoned by years on the sea and in battle. The old pirate came to the young captain with a limp leg and a slow stride brought on by old age and injury. "Are we on the right track?" asked the young captain.

"Aye," replied the elder.

"I'm curious," replied the captain, "just as to why you decided to board my ship."

The older pirate grinned and looked down to the aged wooden planks that formed the deck of the ship. "You refer to my age?" the pirate responded.

"Aye," replied the captain.

"You're young," spoke the elder. "There was a time I stood in your place. When I was a young captain leading my ship on its first treasure hunt- into the world against a sea of a thousand foes." The young captain smiled before returning to the horizon.

"I survived a hundred battles at sea," continued the older pirate. "I raided towns and forts and villas on beaches you have probably never heard of. I mastered the art of the sword and the pistol and danced in the moonlight with men of all walks of life."

The pirate paused in sadness. "I survived," the old pirate continued. "When my carpenter died, and my boatswain passed on, and even the cook left the ranks; I found myself with a crew of men who had no idea who I was. So I left my ship and settled down. I found a nice home on an island overlooking the sea and started a family."

After a brief pause, the young captain worded, "And?"

"I began to see the water on the horizon the way you might see a painting hanging over a fireplace- some strange piece of art that you might walk past a hundred times and never notice. For fifty years, I never even set foot on another boat again."

"And now?" the captain asked.

"All of my family is now either dead or moved away," the elder continued. "In my old shack on the island, I heard a cry for adventure seekers wishing to find riches under a new pirate captain in town. For the first time since retirement, I smelled the salt in the ocean breeze once more. That is why I joined your crew, Captain."

"That's quite the story," the young pirate replied.

The elder of the two turned to meet the younger with an expression of advice. "You're young," the elder spoke. "Take this from someone who has stood in your place before." A pause. "Keep going. From all of us who gave it up and forgot the smell of the sea, keep going; for as long as you can. Because one day- if god forbid you survive the battles and the raids, and the dancing in the moonlight- one day you will forget the smell of the sea, and it is the worst tragedy that can befall someone that stands where you stand."

"So Gone" Monica

I'm looking outside the window of my hostel in Leipzig, struggling over the thought of writing an ethnography that can in and of itself describe the plight of a group of people who have struggled for years to gain acceptance, success, and recognition for their hard work. In previous studies, I wrote about women who had anthropologists before- and greater than- myself who could with less words describe in greater detail their fight for equality. It is with a bit of frustration then, that I found out last summer that one of the world's oldest sports- (fencing was established in Ancient Egypt about five thousand years ago- with equal participation of women alongside the Egyptian men)- has no anthropological research about the experience of women.

In my rookie years as an ethnographer, I joked about being a terrible anthropologist who was lucky to find myself in the right place at the right time with no one more qualified to write the story I found myself a part of. But two years later, I find myself held to a standard to which I am entirely new. In the sport of fencing, women have fought for the simple right to exist- and recently too. Women did not gain full participation rights at the Olympic Games until the Twenty-first Century.

But while the struggle to gain acceptance from a world audience (and in the heavily political realm of international sports), the struggle most women in fencing find is within the confines of their own self. Hidden behind a literal mask designed to defend them from the aggressive attacks of a sword-wielding opponent and within the psychological mask of a swordswoman with legs shaking in exhaustion; in each fencer is a woman struggling just to keep going.

The sport of fencing has no professional level for men or women, and most women I have spoken with are quick to add that men usually face the same struggle that women face; but behind the veil of under-familiarity, these women often later reveal a counter-thesis which describes a struggle in sport unique to women in fencing. Almost every woman in the world- even those not in sports- often find themselves brushed aside when looking for a job or trying to gain acceptance in a society that believes in giving chances to unknown men, but not to unknown women.

Pay too often goes to the more famous actors, athletes, and public figures. For the majority of women fencers, pay can directly relate to their fame- meaning a young girl joining the sport will never receive a penny from their home country to help alleviate the cost of equipment, travel, lodging, and tournament fees. There are few sponsors in fencing- and the few that exist only support famous fencers.

Without paychecks or sponsorships, few women survive in the sport past their thirtieth birthday, and it is around that time that those athletes face their greatest opponent- themselves. With a bank account drained of every dollar (run dry through years of replacing broken swords, bones, and spirits), most fencers have to have a long and life changing (and not in the good way) conversation with themselves about their future. At about thirty years old, most women put away the swords they carried for ten years, pack away their uniforms, and hang their masks one last time before assuming a desk job in some cityscape where the minute hand on the clock has replaced a screeching opponent as their new arch nemesis.

Perhaps in this rare moment, I *am* the most qualified anthropologist to write about these modern warrior women though. Apart from having ten years of fencing experience under my own "mask," I think perhaps I understand the struggle these women face. Looking out the window of my hostel in Leipzig, I contemplate how many times I checked my bank account today. Anthropology, like fencing, is rarely funded. Even with university funding, anthropologists struggle with the deficit of expensive travel costs, student loan payments, and the ever-alluring pull of a boring desk job in a boring city, which pays ten times as much (with dental!).

I don't think I can continue forever. There will be a day when I hang up the beach blanket I got at the nude beach in Canada. There will come a time when my passport collects dust and my backpack finds a new home in my closet. I wanted to use the story of the two pirates to demonstrate the struggle women in fencing face all too often. That at some point- if they survive the injuries sustained in tournaments- one day they will have to put down the sword and find a full-time job sitting at a desk and pressing buttons on a computer all day. And the worst part of all of this is you probably assumed the pirates in the story were men.

"Comportement" Aya Nakamura

The story of women in fencing might seem bleak and

depressing; but in the larger context of the ancient sport, the story of the role of women is like the Russian fairytale of the Firebird- one of life, death, and rebirth. During my time at the Fencing World Championships, I met women competing in their first world championships, their last world championships, and everywhere in between. And even those who had given up the sport found new life in roles as coaches, instructors, and parents to a new generation of women in fencing now representing a proverbial "changing of the guard" as the last line of revolutionary women who brought women's saber to the Olympic Games in 2004 now find themselves retiring from the sport, starting families, and finding new jobs.

Apart from the obvious desire to write about fencing due to my own investment in the sport, I wanted to carve out a piece of history that would otherwise be lost due to the larger anthropological community's disinterest. The last group of women who fenced in the first Olympic Games where women were granted equal access to compete are now out of the game. (Though Mariel Zagunis- the last of the original women's saber fencers- may return after giving birth to her first child). A new generation is now leading the sport into the future as the first non-founding generation of women fencers. This new generation has its own unique obstacle to overcome- paying bills.

I know this obstacle well. At my new job at the high school this past school year; I made fourteen dollars an hour for forty hours a week. After taxes, I made about two thousand dollars a month. I paid four hundred dollars a month in rent, about a hundred fifty in utilities and another hundred fifty in cell phone bills. Then there was the roughly three hundred dollars a month I spent on groceries. By the end of any given month, I had about seven hundred dollars left- and that's if I did absolutely nothing fun.

For women in fencing, their struggle comes at a higher cost. In fencing, there are three categories (called weapons due to the use of different swords) so any given international fencer will likely travel once every three months for an international tournament during a given season (which is a twelve month season, unlike say soccer which is usually five months). Let's say a fencer has to fly from the United States to four international tournaments per year plus the zonal championship (for the US it would be the PanAmerican Games) and the World Championships (let's ignore the Olympics for now)- that's six tournaments with roundtrip flights rarely heading to cheap airport terminals.

The total cost just for flights then is roughly six thousand dollars (if lucky). Then there are hotel costs (let's say a tournament lasts a week, meaning eight nights at a hotel per tournament at about one hundred dollars a night- if lucky). That's about five thousand dollars for the season. Then there's food ($1000 US per year if lucky), transport to and from the tournament venue ($500 US per year if lucky), paying for equipment ($500 US per year if lucky), and tournament entry fees ($3000 US per year if lucky).

That means that on a good year, a fencer can expect to spend sixteen thousand US dollars per year- if lucky. Imagine for a moment having no full-time job from age 18 to 28 (ten years) and paying sixteen thousand dollars per year on a sport you have devoted your entire life to- only to then have to pay on top of that rent, utilities, cell phone bills, groceries, student loans, and health insurance.

My total for these things amounts to about twenty thousand, dollars per year- and that's nothing compared to what people living in major cities would have to pay. So let's just assume say Nzingha Prescod of the United States who lives in New York City manages to find an apartment as affordable as mine in Sitka, Alaska and that all her monthly bills are somehow the same as mine. She would be spending almost $36,000 US per year. (I don't even make that much money at my full-time job.)

Thus, the career of a woman in the sport of fencing is often short lived- not due to the physical cost of athletic endurance, but due to the financial burden of monetary endurance. At some point in every fencer's life they have to deal with the very real issue of choosing between a life they love that is killing their bank account, and a much more boring life that replenishes their bank account. With this dilemma- the ritual of life, death, and rebirth defines the role of women in fencing- and set the stage for 2017 Fencing World Championships in Leipzig, Germany.

While at the airport in Sitka- before departing for my first trip to Europe- I pondered over the question as to why I spend so much of my own money for these adventures. To be entirely honest, nobody buys my books (apart from my mom). I had a moment of pause when I started thinking about why any of it matters. I probably spend about three to five thousand dollars per year on these sports studies. At the end of the day- with all the blood, sweat, and tears (and there are all three of these things every year), I end up defaulting to my full-time job in Sitka as a means of paying for my research.

I then walked through security and headed towards the plane; tucking away that question into the back corners of my mind. After two brief days in Seattle (including a much needed shopping trip for new clothes), I finally boarded my plane for Italy. I had no other choice but to fly to Milan when the cost was two thousand dollars round trip as opposed to four thousand for the roundtrip to Leipzig. So I begrudgingly boarded a plane to Italy and prepared for a week of beaches, cheap wine, and beautiful people. (Anthropology is not an easy job, but somebody has to do it.)

"Giovani fluo" Asia Ghergo

After landing in first Frankfurt, I had both severe jet lag and a five hour layover before my flight to Milan. I found a quiet place to lie down in one of the terminals and took a nap. After my four-hour slumber, I woke up and headed for my flight to Milan. Once there, I ordered a taxi and headed for my hostel. When I got there, I found out I had scheduled the wrong nights for my stay and managed to negotiate a two-night stay including for the night I had arrived. The next morning; I ate breakfast at the hostel, which included strange bagel-shaped crackers and Italian coffee. (Getting real fancy.)

After breakfast, I spoke with the only other guest in my room who was a refuge from Iran. The older man let me ask him about home since I had a friend from college who moved to the US from Iran in her youth. The man was a college-educated engineer who went to school in Iran while the Iranian king was still in power. He came to the US when the king was deposed and struggled to find work with the stigma of his nation of origin. After I told him what I did for a living, he talked about Iran's long history of incredible women who helped shape their role as strong figures of his nation's history- even speaking proudly of women's rights under the monarchy before talking about the oppression under the present regime.

Later that day, I met an old friend and roommate from Florida (who served in AmeriCorps with me in Alaska) for lunch at what would be the third day of a marathon of pizza. (I ate pizza nearly every day during my trip. I might have a problem.) While there, a local family sat next to us and the father became ecstatic when he overheard me talking about women in fencing.

He immediately introduced himself and began talking about how proud he is of the Italian women (like Valentina Vezzali) who have made a name for themselves and for Italy in the sport. But the experience of women fencers in Italy- and for that matter France, Russia, and the United States- is rare. In places like the United Kingdom, Germany, Australia, South Korea, and Mexico; few (if any) people can name women from their country who compete at the international level.

I threw in Valentina Vezzali's name earlier because Vezzali is considered the greatest fencer of all time- for men or women. She won more medals at the Summer Olympics than any other fencer in history, competed at more Olympic Games than any other, and only lost roughly one out of every one thousand bouts in competition. At her inaugural Olympic Games, Vezzali earned the silver medal in 1996, then went on to earn the gold in 2000, 2004, and 2008 before earning the bronze in 2012. She also earned team medals with fellow Italian fencers earning the gold medal in 1996, 2000, 2004, 2008, and 2012. That means by the end of her career, Vezzali earned one bronze medal, one silver, and six gold medals over a span of sixteen years.[14]

Valentina Vezzali is such an important person in the history of fencing that when the Italian fencing team returned from the Leipzig World Championships and met with the president of Italy to receive national awards for their service to the country at the tournament, Vezzali was there to hand out the awards personally. That means Vezzali basically had the same hierarchical position as the president of the country in that moment.

"She was a police officer too!" I excitedly told my friend.

"What?! Really?" he asked.

"Yes," replied the father sitting next to us. "But many Italian Olympians are."

"Wait, really?" I returned; this time being the one surprised.

"Yes, yes," he spoke. "Olympic sports are very expensive. There's travel and accommodations to pay for- and equipment.

Many athletes work in public service like police or military. The Italian government is very understanding too. When an athlete needs to take a break from their job to prepare for the Olympics, they can quit their job, spend a year in sports, then return to work."

With Vezzali- and fencers like her- many work as police officers or soldiers who receive amazing pay and benefits during off-season, then they can put their job on hold to prepare for major events like the Olympics or World Championships. When it's all done, the athlete goes back to being a police officer or soldier. The system must work pretty well too because Italian fencers dominate at the world stage in all three weapons.

After lunch, Tampa (as those who have read my previous books- so my mom- can tell you; I use city names in place of people's names to protect anonymity) and I headed to the Castle in Milan. Tampa explained to me the Castle was a renovated palace converted by the invasive Spanish as a means of intimidation towards the indigenous Milanese as a means of preventing a revolution. The massive piece of architecture lived up to its intimidating design. Cannon holes, tall bastions, and a massive plaza all defined the fortress. But I didn't go to Europe for fancy buildings.

"Si vedono i fiori" Flora

Later that night I met a German woman for beers at a local bar to talk about her experiences in the sport of fencing. After a brief introduction about how she started the sport and why she enjoyed it so much, a Swedish woman joined us (as the former was a

Couchsurfer host in town and would be hosting the Swedish woman). During the German-style drinking session in fashion-forward Milan, I had a hard time getting Mannheim to open up about more of her experiences.

As a male feminist researcher, I have to understand that sometimes women will not feel comfortable sharing particular stories with me, so I usually have to either move past it and leave the stories unheard; or give my own example of a negative experience in the hopes that it will make the other person more comfortable with sharing. In this case I did the latter, talking about an experience of my own which caused me to question quitting the sport of fencing, which- by age eighteen- had become one of the most important things in my life. The plan worked, and Mannheim opened up about sexual harassment she faced during her early teens.

In fencing, women are required to wear an extra piece of safety gear called a chest protector, which resembles a medieval breastplate made out of fiberglass. Since men are not required to wear it, men almost never wear it- setting an early stage for gender division among male and female fencers. When Mannheim was first going through puberty, she had to start wearing a chest protector at practices and the boys in her club would intentionally target her with attacks only a centimeter above the rim of the chest protector as a way of hitting her in the chest where the armor would not protect her.

As the harassment only became worse- with no intervention from coaching or instructor staff- Mannheim decided to quit fencing to escape the harassment, even though fencing had become a staple of her identity. After going through four years of high school without the sport, Mannheim felt fencing luring her back into its ranks and when she started university, she returned to the sport as an instructor.

After I was able to get Mannheim to open up, the three of us continued to talk about sports. I talked about how in the United States; there are a lot of athletic opportunities for kids. Depending on where an American grows up, they have the option of participating in the following list of common sports in US schools: soccer, [American] football, basketball, volleyball, track and field, cross country, swimming, hockey, tennis, golf, field hockey, baseball, softball, and lacrosse. (And those are the popular ones.) In Germany, a student only has two options- soccer or fencing. That means any teenager in Germany who wants to play sports, but doesn't like team sports does fencing. In the United States, fencing is a fringe sport largely populated by outcasts.

To briefly add my own narrative here, I learned how to fence through Boy Scouts; then continued as a Venture Scout- a super niche organization even within the Scouting subculture in the United States. (In actuality, I wanted to do archery instead. This book could have been *much* different.) This is not a unique story either. Most Olympic fencers come from at least some kind of alternative background.

Nzingha Prescod began fencing at nine years old with the Peter Westbrook Foundation in Harlem (a neighborhood of New York City historically populated by working class African-

Americans).[15] Monica Aksamit began fencing at nine years old because she was extremely tall for her age at the time. (So I'm guessing it was either going to be basketball or fencing.)[16]

My personal favorite fencer (I want to preemptively seek forgiveness from all other fencers here. You are all amazing- but the following woman is my favorite because she's the only one out of all of you who actually trained me- even if only for two hours during a guest seminar. So if you want to move up the list, come visit my club in Alaska.) Nicole Ross told my college fencing club during a guest seminar that she got into fencing because she loved the *Princess Bride* and basically forced her parents to find her a fencing club as a nine-year old so that she could be like the characters in the movie.

Somebody much more important than me once said that physics and poetry were the same thing- without later explaining why- and for a long time this equation played in my head as I tried to decipher its meaning. While on the train from Milan to Genoa, I tucked this question into the back corners of my mind while watching the Italian countryside pass behind me. I decided to go to Genoa on a whim. It had absolutely nothing to do with my research; but I was as close to the Mediterranean Sea as I had ever been in my life (and probably ever will be), and I absolutely needed to swim in its waters.

When I arrived in Genoa, I began a slow and sweaty climb to the top of a massive hill towards my hostel; following cryptic descriptions that sounded like something out of a pirate treasure map. (And perhaps for good reason. Genoa is an Italian city founded by pirates.) After passing twelve big white churches (wondering if each one was *the* big white church described in the codex), climbing herculean staircases, crawling up steep brick alleyways, and dodging dodgy cloaked figures; I finally made it to the hostel where I would be staying- and it was well worth the climb.

The hostel was built out of a repurposed castle on a hill. After taking a brief and well-deserved nap and cold shower, I headed into the courtyard of the hostel and immediately found companionship among the other guests. I would end up staying at this hostel for three nights, but those three nights were a lifetime to me. The thing with anthropology is that it's not quite like physics or chemistry or even other social sciences. I don't think a robot could ever replace an anthropologist the way a drill can replace a gold miner or how a calculator could replace a mathematician.

There's an art to anthropology- a human requirement of a real-life person experiencing the world with their own eyes, seeing the world through the eyes of other real-life persons; of asking questions, feeling emotion and empathy- things that no robot could ever reproduce. It is essentially the science not of life (biology) or of space and time (physics) but of living and of place. Anthropology is the science of understanding the human experience- and in that pursuit; a strict adherence to fun is essential. (In other words, I drank... a lot.)

While in Genoa, I went to a beach outside of the city with a group of maybe ten people. We told jokes and drank beer on the train; hiding it in our belief that we might not actually be allowed to drink beer on a train- or that we might be called alcoholics for drinking copious amounts of alcohol at 11am (No you're drunk!). We talked of past travels and plans for the not so distant future.

At the beach, we jumped into the sea and swam in its waters, played Frisbee with strangers, and ate some of the best food we've ever eaten. I remember one of the members of our expedition team taking a photo- that she later sent me- which I will forever keep in my memories. The photo is all of us smiling while soaked in salt water and immersed in new friendship. There's a Walt Whitman poem that plays in my head when looking at this photograph.

Oh me! Oh life! of questions of these recurring,
Of the endless trains of the faithless, of cities fill'd with the foolish,
Of myself forever reproaching myself, (for who more foolish than I,
and who more faithless?)
Of eyes that vainly crave the light, of the objects mean, of the
struggle ever renew'd,
Of the poor results of all, of the plodding and sordid crowds I see
around me,
Of the empty and useless years of the rest, with the rest me
intertwined,
The question, O me! so sad, recurring- What good amid these, O me,
O life?
Answer.
That you are here- that life exists and identity,
That the powerful play goes on, and you may contribute a verse.

Oh Me! Oh Life!
Walt Whitman[17]

I think in life, most people walk through their lives in business clothes with their briefcase attending office meetings and conferences. (And there is nothing wrong with that. To each his/her own as some old dead person once said.) I find no life in that lifestyle- no emotion or passion. And that's why- at least I think- I understand athletes- especially fencers. Athletes in fencing do not get paid. They exhaust their bank accounts to fuel a lifestyle that awards no money to winners and no benefits to the defeated.

Apart from gold medals, there is no tangible object a fencer can return home with to replenish their wallets. It is in every sense a "money pit" in which time and resources are spent with no reciprocal funds. And yet, fencing has its own reciprocal economy measured not in dollars and cents but in emotion- an economy that only those who have taken part in its ritual can understand. But I'll try to explain.

Imagine for a moment, the first time a child jumps into a puddle in the rain. Think about how raw that emotion is, how beautiful. Think of the cries of joy and the unbroken laughter. Image now, the first time you truly fell in love or felt your heart brake when it ended. Think about how powerless you felt in that moment. Imagine the deepest emotions of success, of loss- when you dedicated yourself to something impossible and found yourself victorious, or when you knew you could do something and suddenly found yourself defeated.

Before you let these memories disappear, find a mirror and look at yourself. Look at the stories that your eyes alone tell of your past accomplishments and of your anxiety towards your future- of goals reached and obstacles yet to overcome. That image you see, that face, those eyes, that little glimmer of emotion you've just found- I guarantee- is the same way in which athletes in fencing see themselves. That is the economy of emotion- something that no amount of pay or prize money could ever translate. (But maybe someone should still pay these women.)

There's a secret fencers have found- I think- that most people could live their entire lives without learning- financial mortality. As his or her money drains, every fencer knows it won't last forever. Their life in sport must end one day and eventually they will have to settle down and get a job- and maybe even start a family. And yet, with the looming harbinger of death, there precedes life. Every fencer treats each World Championship like it's their last- even if it's their first. They expose their true self from behind their mask, armor, and uniform and expel unfiltered emotion- and the only way for me to see the world the way women in fencing see it was for me to approach the 2017 Fencing World Championships with the exact same world view.

"Christine" Christine and the Queens

While crossing into the Swiss Alps en route to Geneva, I looked back at some of my preliminary research. As I wrote earlier, there is no real ethnography of the sport of fencing- for men or women. There are no major memoirs by famous women in fencing (such as Valentina Vezzali or Mariel Zagunis). Thus, my research- at least I felt- had to not only describe the present of the sport of fencing but the past as well.

Imagine for a moment flipping through pages of some historical photography notebook and seeing powerful women wielding swords and battling foes from not just the Twenty-first or Twentieth Centuries, but from a thousand years ago to the present; and there are no names to go with any image in that book. No one looking at that book of images of powerful women remember their names. As a historian, I was intent on finding those names.

I could start with the time of Joan of Arc- a woman that probably laid the foundation for women in fencing in France; a woman who picked up the sword and demanded equal participation in combat with the men and who proved herself a capable swordswoman. I could perhaps begin the list with Mary Reed and Anne Bonny- two pirates who swash-buckled their way across the Caribbean Sea and put fear in the hearts of those who crossed them (but you could reread the introduction for that).

While these were certainly powerful women who had powerful sword work, they do not quite embody the culture of the sport of fencing (though if you want to read about these women and others, I highly suggest you educate yourself), so instead I want to start with Gladys Davies- a name probably no one has ever heard of- and a name that I really could not find any information on except one; Gladys Davies (from Great Britain) won the silver medal in the 1924 Olympic Games in the women's individual foil event.

This was the first year any women ever competed in fencing at the Olympics- a time when women still wore dresses and skirts in the sport instead of the gender non-conforming "pants." (Actually, this is a good time to throw some knowledge your way. Fencing pants have different names depending on where you go. They can either be called *knickerbockers* by the romantic philosophers, *trousers* by the classical folk, or simply *fencing pants* by more modern fencers.) Her fellow medal winners that year were Ellen Osiier who won the gold medal and Grete Heckscher who won the bronze (both from Denmark).[18]

More than fifty years later, the second individual fencing event was opened at the Olympics for female competitors. (As in after 1924, it took the International Olympic Committee until 1996 to finally think it was okay for women to have two thirds of what men had instead of only one third). At the 1996 Atlanta Olympic Games, Laura Flessel of France took the gold in women's individual epee. Valerie Barlois (France) took the silver, and Gyongyi Szalay (Hungary) took the bronze.[19]

Finally in 2004, the IOC began questioning whether women only having 66% of what men have might not be such a cool thing after all and allowed women to compete in all fencing events at the Olympics in which men compete. (Good call, guys. A little late, but good call.) In 2004, the first women to receive medals in women's individual saber were Mariel Zagunis (United States), Tan Xue

(China), and Sada Jacobson (United States).[20]

Of all nine of these women, only one of them was competing as of 2017. That makes Mariel Zagunis the last, first Olympic medal winner in women's fencing who still wields a sword in international competition. I remember a moment in Vancouver during my soccer study when I met a waitress at a bar who was a soccer player when she was in college.

I asked her why she stopped playing soccer after graduating, and her response was, "I had to get a job."

Men deal with the crippling dilemma of quitting sports to pursue a career at a desk just as women do, but women face extra scrutiny for extending their athletic careers. As I learned during my rodeo study, a woman in rodeo (cowgirl) is often criticized for competing in rodeos after she starts having children because she is seen as a mother first and an athlete second- and she would be abandoning her family to compete in sports. A male rodeo athlete (cowboy) is often seen as an athlete first and a father second- so he would just be doing his job by leaving his family to compete. (In fact, many would celebrate a cowboy who retired from sport to raise his family, which would be a requirement for respect for women.)

Women who cross over into their thirties in fencing are almost expected to quit. (How dare this maternally aged lady play sports?!) To make things harder, most fencers (men and women) are financed not by victorious medal winning (like in tennis or rodeo) nor through sponsorships (although it does rarely happen), but through mom and dad who usually pay for their kids' competitions.

Just like with every money-hole venture in life, there comes a day when mom and dad stop paying for their kids' adventures- and that is unfortunately when a fencer usually retires from their sport. (If you're wondering how Mariel Zagunis pays for competition, she is one of the rare fencers of the world who does have a sponsor.)

There's a film that came out in the 1980's about immortal sword fighters who formed a group of original swordsmen known as the Highlanders (as the film was called *Highlander*) and the whole plot revolved around there eventually coming a day when only one Highlander would be left standing- the last of an original line of immortal beings. So Mariel, if you are reading this, you are the Highlander of fencing. You are the last, first Olympic fencer in the history of the sport to retire. (You can collect your broadsword if you ever visit Sitka, Alaska.)

When I got to Geneva, I arrived at almost midnight to find a futuristic building vastly different to the castle I stayed at in Genoa. All doors were automatic and the youth in the dining room area were taking shots of Jagermeister instead of slowly enjoying wine. After checking in, I sat down with a glass of water and watched the college party style atmosphere around me before heading to bed. The next morning, the place was empty- as I imagined the partiers from the night before were extremely hung over. I ate breakfast while my laundry went through the machines in the basement of the hostel and enjoyed the quiet of the early morning.

While going down to switch my laundry into the dryers, a young Swedish man was folding his own laundry fresh out of the machines. We got to talking and I learned that this was his first time leaving Scandinavia and he told me all about his plans for his big European trip. While it was certainly my first European trip as well, I saw a former version of myself in Stockholm- one of myself before I graduated from college and when I first went on vacation by myself to New Orleans for a concert. It was my first solo adventure into the world. Later that day, Stockholm and I met back up at the hostel's dining room and headed into the city to meet a Couchsurfer to explore the city.

The adventure would find us playing chess on a life-sized board- and of course I won. We had ice cream, sat with our feet in a Calvinist fountain, met with other strangers (in said fountain), and finally raced to a park to watch an outdoor movie. The film was called *Pride* and centered around a 1980's group of gay and lesbian activists trying to raise donations for a group of Welsh coal miners on strike.

There was a moment in the film where the representative of the miners' strike first met with the activist group who invited him to come out to a gay bar with them after their initial meeting. He was asked to deliver a speech to the club- and after a bit of confusion over just what to say- told the audience, "There's no greater feeling in the world than finding a friend you never knew you had..." before expressing his thanks on behalf of his miners.

The quote stuck with me. When I was growing up, I played a lot of sports over the years (soccer, track and field, volleyball, tennis, kayaking, canoeing, riflery, archery, rock climbing, etc.) but fencing was the only sport I ever felt I belonged in- and maybe because it was due to the friendliness of the sport. I could have homeschooled kids and kids from other high schools in the same club as me. I got to know them better than I knew kids at my own school. I met fencers from all over the country- and in some cases foreign countries- and became their friends as well. (In fact, one of my friends from fencing who was only ever an opponent was one of five people who took me out drinking on my twenty-first birthday.)

This is not unique to the United States. Across the world, most people join fencing because- for one reason or another- they didn't fit in with other sports. In Germany and the UK, fencers told me they did fencing because it was either soccer or fencing, and they couldn't play team sports. In the United States, fencing is a haven for nerdy kids who want to play sports, but because their high school didn't have quidditch, they went with fencing. In many Muslim communities, fencing is a rare sport where even the more conservative women and girls can participate due to the fashion of the sport.

While I'm at it, I should take the time to actually describe the fashion of fencing because- like my hostel in Geneva- fashion in fencing is not only sleek and fancy, but also balances old styles with new mechanics. From toe to head (ignoring undergarments because we know what's going on there) a fencer must wear tennis shoes, knee-high socks, knickerbockers/trousers/fencing pants, an undershirt, a plastron (a thick cotton piece resembling half of a t-shirt where only one side of the body is covered), a chest protector (required for women and suggested for men), a thick cotton jacket, a lamé (A lamé for foil is shaped like a vest while a lamé for saber is shaped like the jacket, and there is none for epee.), a glove for the sword-hand, and a mask.

With all of this gear, the only body parts visible are one hand and the hair on the fencer's head. (And in the case of some women and men with long hair, they will occasionally wear a hat to cover their hair in order to keep it out of their eyes under the mask.) This all means that fencing is a rare sport where the uniform falls in line with conservative Islamic dress code. There should be no surprise then for anyone who understands the uniform to learn that some of the best female fencers in the world are Muslim or come from Muslim countries- for example Ibtihaj Muhammad of the United States or Sarra Besbes of Tunisia.

Along with all of this gear, each fencer is required to have a minimum of two swords, two body chords, and two mask chords (the latter of which is not used for epee). Under the sleeves of the plastron, jacket, and lamé- each fencer has an electrical chord that on one side plugs into an outlet attached to the sword and on the other side plugs into a circuit connected- either through a wireless system or through another set of chords run through a pulley system- to the scoring machine.

Foils and epees both have buttons on the tip of the sword with a thin wire running from the tip of the blade to the socket at the handle. When the button is pressed, an electric signal runs through all of the electrical circuits to the scoring machine to show a touch on the button on the sword. The saber is an electric circuit in and of itself thus allowing any part of the blade to touch an opponent to signal the scoring machine. Mask chords connect the mask of a fencer to the circuit as well.

Now if all of this seems confusing, it might be because- as far as I know- fencing is the only sport of its kind to do something so futuristic. Imagine for a second that every American football player had wires sticking out of them that ran all the way across the field. Every time a player was tackled, some light would go off on the side of the field, and the play would stop for the referees to judge.

Or think about a tennis player having an electric racket that could light up every time the ball hit the netting. (This one actually sounds pretty cool.) Fencing is a sport invented by the Ancient Egyptians about three thousand years ago- and somehow it is the only sport in which athletes are momentarily cybernetic organisms combining anatomically modern humans and electrically engineered mechanics. (I will let you pause here to think about how badass that is.)

To make things even more sci-fi; fencers fence on what is referred to as a "pisté" aka a "strip." This is a thin line six feet wide and forty-five feet long, which acts as the court on which fencers compete. At special fencing tournaments like the Olympics or the World Championships, these strips have their own lights and electronic parts. In fact, at the Leipzig Games- one fencing equipment manufacturer unveiled a new prototype pisté made up of thousands of tiny lights that would light under a fencer's feet to track foot movement. (This puts the racquetball court my club practices on to shame.)

Before the movie began in the park in Geneva, the group I arrived with met with an even larger group enjoying a picnic. One of the group members was a physicist from CERN working on the Large Hadron Collider. I told him about the quote tying physics and poetry together and asked him if it were true, "… how are physics and poetry the same thing?"

After thinking about the answer for about fifteen minutes, he gave me his answer. "I'm not sure if this will make sense," he started, "but- at least in my mind- mathematics is the language of the universe. So, in a way, physics is how the universe expresses itself- because as poetry is how people express themselves with English or French, or whatever language; that's physics. Physics is poetry written by the universe using the language of mathematics." I loved his answer- and told him I loved his answer.

Part of what drew me to fencing was not its sci-fi element or its conservative dress (although, I have to admit, I feel complete only when in full fencing gear with a sword in my hand). It's because no matter where in the world a fencer goes to compete; a bout always ends with a salute and a handshake. It's because when a fencer scores an incredible point doing something over-the-top badass, their opponent is the first person to give them a high five. There's an unspoken bond among fencers that does not exist in other sports, and that human connection- under all the cybernetic parts, under the armor, and under the protective gear soaked in the worst smelling sweat stains a person will ever smell (seriously though, fencer sweat is the worst)- defines the culture of fencing.

Chapter 2: Lunge

"Planes, Trains, Automobiles" Julia Wu

To better understand what fencers around the world share in common, I wanted to first learn more about fencers from different countries. Before heading to Europe, I got in contact with some women from the United States who competed at the national level in saber before the event was added to the Olympic roster. Both women fenced at the NCAA level in college, which- at the time- was essentially the highest level of competition for women's saber in the United States. When my train emptied in Stuttgart- and after I checked into my new hostel- I looked over the results of these interviews.

One of the women stated that she started fencing later than most collegiate fencers start- as a high school student. She told me a story about how she was playing basketball, but really did not enjoy it. When she found the kids practicing fencing in the cafeteria, she wanted to switch to fencing almost immediately. She reported the group was an "oddball collection of individuals," which she felt "very at home with." The other woman started as a nine year-old who met with early success in fencing, which was essential for her enjoyment of the sport.[21]

When asked about unique rituals that set their clubs apart from others, one of the women recalled her club's ritual of stealing weird things from competitors (or I suppose raiding might be the right word here), which included at least once a bench from Harvard's locker room. The other recalled less pirate-like rituals related to warming up and psyching themselves up before competitions.[22]

Both agreed on how translatable the language and lessons of fencing can be for young people. Beyond the universal concepts of dealing with defeat and being respectful in victory, fencing requires a massive amount of fast thinking. It requires an ability to read body language as a means of predicting the immediate future. Some people often connect fencing and chess- often nicknaming fencing "physical chess." I never actually thought that was correct though, and many fencers also dissent on the analogy.

For me, fencing was more like sudoku with a three-minute time limit. Each box only has a limited number of options, and a person can decipher which numbers go where depending on context clues presented by preexisting numbers. But on a time limit, a person has to be fluent in reading the numbers on the page and take serious risks in guessing what to put where in order to finish in time. That's how fencing works.

In the sport of fencing, there are only three things a fencer can do on their feet- move forward (known as advance), move backward (known as retreat) or launch themselves forward (known as a lunge). There are only nine attacks (though in each weapon, there are only ever really four or five that are used- and these five differ for each weapon), and nine defenses (known as parries). Just like sudoku, there are a massive number of possibilities that result from the combination of nine attacks, nine defenses, and three-foot movements. And a good fencer has to be able to make split-second decisions as to how to combine these three things in order to win in their sport.

I also spoke with two internationals- Manon Brunet of France and Martina Criscio of Italy- who told me more about their experiences in fencing. (I was disappointed at the lack of locker room raid stories from these two.) Both began fencing at eight years old. Brunet of France told me that before joining, she tried various other sports (including taekwondo) before ending up in fencing. Both started first with foil before entering saber later on.[23]

In fencing, there are three categories for competition (much like the way track and field has different events) known as *weapons*. These are foil, epee, and saber. Most people who start fencing begin with foil- and this aspect of the sport in and of itself is a long tradition. Fencing as a sport itself is a sport of tradition. In fact, most fencing coaches are known as *Maestro* or *Master* instead of coach or instructor. Each of the three different weapons in fencing derives from three different origins. Foil- the weapon most people begin with when first starting in the sport- derived as a training weapon. (Thus the training weapon is still used today in fencing as the training weapon. Simple and easy to remember.)

Foil came about during the Medieval Period when infantry were given cheap swords to use on the battlefield. Since infantry were likely to die fairly quickly (the literal pawns of Medieval warfare- in that the pawn chess piece is historically derived from

Medieval infantry), most weapon smiths did not want to waste time or resources on weapons that would end up in a dead man's hands. Thus these swords were lightweight, usually short, and could only penetrate simple armor with simple stabs.

These infantry were trained to use this sword with minimal effort- often simply telling soldiers to aim for the lungs and the kidneys of their opponent. These four targets (two lungs and two kidneys) are now the primary targets for attack in foil fencing. The sword itself is the most lightweight of the three weapons, and attacks are usually simple lunges or extensions of the arm.

This may also be a good time to interject with information about my lack of source references in the above paragraph. Fencing- as per tradition- is a sport largely of oral history. Growing up in the sport, a young athlete might be training with a maestro who learned their knowledge from someone who trained them, and *that* maestro learned it from someone who trained them.

Snippets of oral history often get thrown in- like the story about foil's origin- with little to know written record. The very concept that I myself am writing a book on fencing actually goes against the tradition of the sport, so we'll see if USA Fencing decides to not renew my membership this season. Thus, there will be times I refer to unique facts about the sport that have no source added to them, and it is due to the fact that it is a story my own "maestro" aka dad told me.

After a year or two, most fencers will usually begin exploring the other two weapons and after finding one they like, they will commit to training in only that weapon. Both Criscio and Brunet committed to saber by the time they were old enough to seriously compete in the sport.[24] Saber is a weapon derived from- as you can probably guess- sabers. The saber (or sabre as more traditionalists like to spell) is a cavalry sword meaning it was used by horse-mounted troops.

While in the saddle, the saddle itself would protect riders from attacks to the groin, legs, and feet. Thus the target for saber is everything above the waist. (In foil, the target also includes the groin- because infantry were not trained to be polite.) The sport of saber derived as a way to train cavalry officers how to fight if they ever fell off their horse. The cavalry saber utilizes the blade of the sword as a weapon instead of just the tip, and so in saber the side of the sword can be used to gain points. (This is the only weapon where this is permitted.)

Even though I did not speak with any international epeeists, I will go ahead and describe epee's origin here as well. (Since I'm already at 66% at this point.) Epee is the only weapon of the three that actually derived from dueling. While foil and saber were military weapons (infantry and cavalry respectively), epee was a civilian weapon used by aristocrats in Renaissance Europe for duels.

Duels during this time were not fought until one person was dead- as most historical dramas would lead their audience members to believe. Duels were fought to what is known as *first blood*, which meant that the first person to bleed lost the duel. If both people bled first simultaneously, the duel was called as a draw or tie. In epee, if two people hit at the same time, they both get a point- and this is unique to epee. (Foil and saber have a *right of way* system I will explain later.)

Also, the button on the tip of the epee is stiffer than for foil. The amount of pressure it would take to depress the button on an epee is the exact same amount of pressure it would take for a sharp tip to penetrate the skin and make a person bleed. (Tradition!) Also, since there were no rules as to where on the body a scar had to appear for a duelist to lose, epee is the only weapon of the three in which the entire body is a target. (As in toes, knees, and pinky fingers are all fair game.)

While in Stuttgart, I managed to maintain a strict ritual of waking up, getting coffee in the hostel lounge, taking notes on articles, getting lunch in the hostel lounge (with a beer), taking a nap, waking up, drinking another coffee in the afternoon, taking notes on more articles, getting dinner in the hostel lounge (with *two* beers), taking more notes on more articles, then going to bed. In the two nights I was in Stuttgart, I never left the hostel. But my loyalty to agoraphobia paid off. The bartender who worked in the hostel lounge enjoyed asking me questions about women in fencing and enjoyed bragging about his country's women's national soccer team- so much so that he usually gave me a free beer each night.

After two nights in Stuttgart, I boarded another train and headed to Leipzig for the World Championships. Most of the athletes at this time were sharing similar experiences. After a week of intense training ahead of the tournament, various athletes began taking to social media to report on their two days of freedom before the big event. French fencer Ysaora Thibus referred to this as "The calm before the storm," with an instagram update. Italian fencer Rossella Fiamingo posted videos of pre-game dancing and ice cream, and Martina Criscio posted images of her road trip through Italy. After two days of pregame R&R, my train pulled out of the station in Stuttgart and headed towards Leipzig.

My train towards Leipzig required a layover in Frankfurt with only a small window of time between switching trains. As my train unloaded in Frankfurt, I immediately rushed to the platform where my next train would finally bring me to Leipzig. While standing on the platform waiting for the train to pull in, I saw a beautiful woman. When the train pulled in, she immediately boarded, and I somehow managed to end up sitting next to her.

(*Somehow in this context meant that I boarded the car in front of hers to find her leaving her car and following *me* towards where I was sitting. So don't think for a second I was creeping my way across Europe for a month.) As the train departed the station, I followed it on my mobile map to estimate how soon I would be in Leipzig only to find out the train was heading back towards Stuttgart. When the ticket checker came by to look at our tickets, I panicked. Luckily, the man spoke fluent English and helped me figure out what went wrong and told me which station to get off at. To even greater luck, the cute girl seated next to me spoke fluent English as well.

"Are you lost?" she asked.

"Uhhhhh," I uttered in nervousness. "Yeah, I guess I am." (In reality, I wasn't, but when a beautiful local woman offers to give me directions; I accept those directions one hundred percent of the time.)

"Where are you from?" she asked.

"Alaska," I replied.

"Wait, really?" she asked. "Do you know Wasilla?" she continued.

"Are you serious?" I responded confusedly. "Of course I know Wasilla! How do you know where Wasilla is?"

The woman started telling me a story about how she did a student exchange program in 2009 while in high school at a school in Wasilla (a small town outside of Anchorage, Alaska for those uneducated in Alaska geography), and we started talking about life in the state which I now call home. Wasilla helped find me a train that would take me from the station I would be dropped off at that would bring me all the way to Leipzig. After exchanging instagram contacts, I left the train and Wasilla wished me luck catching the next one.

On the next train, I managed to follow directions and got on the right train this time to find yet another beautiful woman opting to sit next to me. (Europe, you're amazing.) This woman was a veterinarian from Uruguay who also spoke near-fluent English-though I felt the need to speak Spanish at some points. Eventually I made it to Leipzig on time, but it is important for me to note that in anthropology; few plans ever become reality.

It is common for someone trying to take a train from Stuttgart to Leipzig (metaphorically of course) to get on the wrong [metaphorical] train. Some people might get anxious and upset and even a little scared as to what to do next. But a well-trained anthropologist not only performs well and calmly under such stressful situations, but also enjoys them. I met two incredible women- an airline steward from Germany and a veterinarian from Uruguay who were both incredibly generous and incredibly badass- and I never would have met them if I took the correct train.

"Non non non (Ecouter Barbara)" Camelia Jordana

My first twenty-four hours in Leipzig however were not as easy. I ended up making it to my hostel in time and went almost immediately to sleep upon arriving after an exhausting trip across the country. After waking up, I left the hostel in the morning to collect my press badge and informational packet from the arena where the fencing tournament would take place. The story of what unfolded there requires its own preface.

In May, I saw that it was free to apply for press accreditation for the event. I had never actually had press access at any of my previous studies (sitting with the audience at the Women's World Cup and at rodeos), but since it was free to apply; I figured it wouldn't hurt to try. The application process required that I upload a photo for my badge, fill out my name and home nation, and list the organization I represented.

The problem is I wasn't representing any organization. But it was a required field in the application process, so I decided to type the name of my website- which in all seriousness is a legitimate website that highlights feminist history, but is also called "Wonder Woman Wednesday." I remember distinctly uttering under my breath while filling the application out, "There's no way these guys are going to say yes."

Two days later, I received an email telling me my application was approved. Two months later, I was in line at the Arena Leipzig to collect my press badge when the staff told me they couldn't find it and had to look up my name in their system. Evidently, I was actually *denied* access to the tournament's press corps because they thought I was a spammer- and every journalist who applied was given an accidental email within 48 hours of their appliance telling them they were approved.

I was suddenly thrust into a situation in which I had to prove that I was in fact an anatomically modern human with human parts, that my website was in fact a legitimate website, that my research was in fact legitimate feminist anthropology, and that I was in fact deserving of the highly coveted press badge. (It didn't help that even I didn't believe any of that.) Luckily, the venue decided to approve of my press accreditation and I walked back to my hostel with a newly printed press badge. (Like a freaking champ!)

I feel the need to be an honest field researcher and anthropologist- even though the American Anthropological Association will probably ban me for life after this. After getting the second email, my immediate thought was, "Well I'll just delete that second email, and show them the original; and if they asked if I got a second email, I'll lie and say no."

I felt pretty good about that plan until I actually started talking to the tournament organizers when I realized they might ask if I had a work visa or special travel visa to be at the tournament for my book. I usually adhere to a strict "Don't make too many waves" policy while on field studies because I'm not quite sure if I actually need special permission to research these topics in foreign countries- and at airport customs I usually just tell the officials that I'm traveling "To watch some sports."

While the middle-aged German woman at the arena questioned me about my accreditation, I feared at best they would take my photo and ban me from entering the arena- and at worst call the police and fly me back to the US. Luckily, my luck lasted longer than my deodorant and I walked away with a press badge. (So any of you would be anthropologists reading this- learn from my mistake.)

I was not the only person though- vying for an opportunity to gain entrance to the 2017 Fencing World Championships. In fencing, the top one hundred twenty-eight athletes in the world in each event (weapon) for each gender (men and women) were permitted to compete in the tournament. Those athletes had to qualify for this position through a combination of overall international rankings and performance in zonal championships (for example the PanAmerican Games).

Those in the top thirty-two positions were automatically in the tournament while those ranked 65-128 had to qualify on site for entrance into the round of sixty-four. On the first two days of the tournament, men and women from around the world competed for the opportunity to compete in the main tournament through participation in "pools" for the round of one hundred twenty-eight in each gender/weapon category for the individual events.

In most fencing tournaments, each event is broken down into two sections- the pools round and the direct elimination round. In the pools round, fencers are placed into groups of anywhere between five and seven athletes who must fence each person in their "pool" in a bout. These "pool bouts" have both a time limit and a score limit. If at any time one fencer reaches five points- that fencer wins the bout and the bout ends. Alternatively- if three minutes of game time pass without either fencer reaching five points, the fencer with the highest score wins the bout. (In saber, there is no time limit- and I will explain why later on.)

In direct elimination bouts, there are three rounds of three minutes each with a one minute break between each round- making for a total of nine minutes of game time. Two athletes fence until one reaches fifteen total points or whoever has the highest score at the end of those three rounds. In saber there is no time limit and there are only two rounds. Fencers compete until one reaches eight total points, then there is a one-minute break, then the bout continues until one fencer reaches fifteen total points.

One of these athletes trying to qualify in the pools round was a seventeen year-old girl named Freya Clarke from Australia. After qualifying for entrance into the round of sixty-four, I spoke with

Freya and her mom in the stands as they watched other bouts in the arena. Freya explained to me how she was the only Australian woman who qualified for the tournament for her event (foil), and that it took a lot of resources for her to make it to Germany to compete. After she left to change out of her gear, her mom spoke to me more about the pressure her daughter was under.

"Nobody back home really cares," her mom told me.

"Really?" I asked surprisingly.

"She doesn't get any recognition," her mom spoke. "Not even her high school cares that she's competing at this high of level." Freya's mom then continued to talk about how difficult it was just to get her daughter into the World Championships. The zonal tournament- the Asian Games- brought female fencers in from Korea, China, and Turkey- all countries with strong female fencers. Freya was able to qualify for world championships among some of the best fencers in the world.

On top of that, Freya and her mom then had to finance their trip to Leipzig out of pocket. The Australian government financed the men's foil team because they performed well at the Rio Olympics, but the government gave only pocket change to Freya and other Australian women at the tournament. (The equivalent of $500 US per female athlete, which is not even enough to pay for half of a plane ticket.)

"You know," Freya's mom added near the end of the conversation. "She doesn't even want to be famous." Her mom paused. "But it would be nice for people to at least notice her. To notice how much she's accomplished just by being here." And with that, Freya returned from changing out of her gear. We said goodbye to each other and I wished Freya good luck in the tournament before they left.

The message Freya's mom told me stuck with me. It was in all regards the exact reason why three years ago I started this long journey into feminist anthropology. There is such a rich history of women who have achieved immeasurably powerful feats, but- due to a series of reasons (aka sexism)- many of these women's names have been either forgotten or erased from history books. At seventeen years old Freya Clarke of Sydney, Australia qualified for the 2017 Leipzig Fencing World Championships. She made it as far as the round of 64, and- at the end of the whole tournament- she was the one athlete I was most proud to have met.

"La canzoni fanno male" Marianne Mirage

On the first official day for women's individual foil, Sabrina Massialas of the United States was struggling with a broken foot in an attempt to break into the round of thirty-two. During one bout, Massialas fell on the strip- barely able to stand on even one leg. After medical staff strapped her ankle with an entire role of medical tape, Massialas attempted to continue. After managing to "karate kid" her way through the first round, she was forced to abdicate and withdrew from the tournament to the applause of a respectful crowd.

Massialas' story was not unique either. There were a lot of injuries at the tournament and the majority of them were with female athletes. Now, a person's immediate response to this might be to assume that female anatomically modern humans have weaker bone structures than males- or that perhaps they have weaker muscles or some other assumption based on biology and anatomy that would support their own subconscious sexism. That person could not be more wrong. Across sports, women often meet more injuries than their men counterparts due to the social pressures of sport.

If a male athlete takes an injury and walks off the field, most people salute that player as a wounded hero. When a female athlete takes an injury that forces them off the field, they fall into the stereotype of women being weak. (You can learn all about this in literally every book I have or will ever write about women's sports because it comes up in every sport.) This is why a male fencer will sustain a minor injury and wave over the medical staff while a female fencer might be in the middle of a bursting appendix and refuse to leave before the end of the round.

A few days later, I somehow managed to sit next to the general manager for Team USA. I asked her how Massialas was recovering and she revealed that the fencer had entered the tournament with an already broken foot- meaning Massialas entered the World Championships with at least one broken bone. I waited until the manager left to utter under my breath, "Sabrina, go to the hospital."

On day one, I actually sat with multiple moms. (I should add here that I met the most success in trying to speak with athletes by first speaking with their mom- and almost every fencer's mom was at the tournament.) At one point, I spoke with US saber fencer Jeff Spear's mom during one of US foil fencer Margaret Lu's bouts. Spear came by to talk to his mom and it turned into a three-way conversation about my work. There was one thing Spear told me that made me think about my research.

"I almost think," he said, "that the stories of the people who *almost* won are the most fascinating."

He explained that especially in women's fencing, there were so many incredible women saber fencers before women's saber was in the Olympics- meaning that there was really nobody around who cared enough to record their stories. There are also a lot of fencers who are in the top ten in their weapon in the world who do not get to compete at the Olympics even today.

Only a max of two fencers per gender per weapon per country may compete in the individual events in fencing at the Olympics, which means if a woman is ranked fourth in the world and third in her country, she is not allowed to compete at the Olympics. Since nations like Italy, Russia, France, and the United States all have numerous and highly ranked women in fencing; the vast majority of the best fencers in the world never even compete at the Olympic Games.

This situation ended up screwing over US foil fencer Nicole Ross who was ranked third in the United States just before the Rio Olympics but who was denied access to compete at the games. After the Olympics, she ended up consistently ranking in the top eight in the world in international competitions between the Rio Olympics and the Leipzig World Championships. At the Cancun World Cup in October 2016, Ross took the bronze medal.[25]

At the World Cup in St. Maur, Ross took the silver medal.[26] At the Turin Grand Prix, Ross again took the silver medal.[27] In fact, of the eight Grand Prix's and World Cups for women's foil in the 2016/2017 season, Ross medaled in three tournaments with top eight finishes in most. In comparison, Inna Deriglazova who earned the gold medal for Russia at the Rio Olympics medaled in the same season as Ross only four times. (That means, the top Olympic foil fencer of the season only made the semifinals fifty percent of the time- only once more than Ross for the season.)

This made me seriously think about who and what I would actually end up writing about in my study. The reason why it was so hard for me to find historical women in fencing is because it is- even for the top fencers in the world- a sport of people who *almost* gained immortal status. While there are certainly fencers like the Nadi brothers (two Italian Olympians from the 1930's considered by some to be the greatest fencers of all time), Valentina Vezzali (the actual greatest fencer of all time), and Mariel Zagunis.

The sport itself is not one of sponsored swordswomen with the planning and financing committees of soccer. It's a sport of women who- along with their parents- pay out of pocket for a chance at one singular moment of glory in a sport where names are quickly forgotten, success is rarely acknowledged, and where the medal podium is made up of men and women who don't consistently place.

In the Pre-Christian Greek religion, the mythological history of the world was divided among three groups of beings- the time of the gods (defined by the war between the Olympians and the Titans), the time of the demi-gods (defined by the stories of Herakles, Perakles, and Jason), and the time of the mortal heroes (defined by the Trojan War).

Like with the mythological history of Ancient Greece, fencing too is a history of mythological figures. The old guard defined as the original Olympians of each weapon and gender has only one being still among the ranks of fencers today- Mariel Zagunis (the Highlander as I described her earlier). The second wave of greats who helped define the masters of the sport (such as the Valentina Vezzali and Laura Flessel) now command powerful roles in government in their home nations of Italy and France- respectively.

Now is the era of heroes in fencing- the mortal beings burdened with the very mortality of their economic status in a sport where almost no one gets paid. There was a golden moment however when seated by Yana Egorian- a Russian saber fencer- in the stands, when a little girl came up to her and nervously asked her to sign a t-shirt the girl had bought at the tournament. Egorian smiled and signed the shirt for her young fan.

At the heart of it all, that is why women's fencing is so important- and why women's sports in general are so important. These women- from Mariel Zagunis to Freya Clarke- inspire young women and girls in ways no desk jockey in a New York City office could ever experience. A simple autograph on a ten Euro t-shirt was enough for Egorian to help show that little girl how incredible women in sports can be- how many young girls one woman can inspire through athletic feats that prove just how badass women can be.

After Sabrina Massialas withdrew from the tournament, all other US women foil fencers were finished for the day. It was also about lunchtime, so I used the momentary pause as an excuse to leave the venue and find some pizza. (The marathon continued.) It was especially hot that day in Leipzig, so I fanned myself in the pizza parlor with my handkerchief as I waited for my pizza to come with my sole companion- a tall glass of beer. After eating some of the best pizza in my life- and drinking a second beer of course- I rushed over to the barbershop across the street for a much-needed haircut and shave.

I should note here that whenever people asked me where I was from on my trip, I would tell them Alaska. "Oh wow," everybody would say, "You're the first person I've met who's from Alaska!"

It's a lot of pressure being someone's first Alaskan. I didn't even grow up there, and even further- the area of Alaska I live in isn't really Alaska. Southeast Alaska is more like Olympia, Washington than Denali; so I don't even consider myself a true Alaskan. With that being said, my facial hair at the time thought otherwise. It was long, scraggly, and could frighten away grizzly bears if necessary. It needed to go.

After sitting down in the barbershop, I quickly discovered the barbers only spoke German and Turkish, which led to one of the most frightening moments of my life. Now, I've stared down territorial bison in Yellowstone, met a mother brown bear protecting her two cubs in the wilds of Alaska, and have been on the top of a mountain during a thunderstorm- none of those compared to this Turkish barber when his hair clippers went straight for my eyebrows.

The *Jaws* theme played in my head as I prayed for any available deity of hair to give me my eyebrows back. Luckily, someone answered in the form of a one-inch filter on those clippers. The barber continued to give me one heck of a haircut and trimmed my beard nicely. For all three cranial haircuts, it only cost fifteen Euros. (One more disaster averted in the books!)

After the terror of the Turkish barber, I decided I needed a nap (which really means after two thick beers at lunch, I needed a nap.) I went back to the hostel and laid my head down on the bed. When I woke up, I headed back to the arena for the opening ceremony and sat with a German fencing club visiting for the weekend to watch the tournament.

Leipzig is known historically as an important city in the narrative of classical music (blah blah blah, I came here for sword stabbing!) so the opening ceremony was marked by a classical music concert and included a ring of flag-bearing children who were largely under qualified for their jobs. One of the kids was casually trying to hide the fact that he forgot his flag.

Another boy struggled to hold the weight of the Brazil flag

while trying to hide the fact that he desperately needed to use the restroom (failing to do either). While in Genoa, a group of Finnish girls introduced me to the term "struggle bus" referring to a person struggling in life. This young flag bearer was on the front seat of that struggle bus, and of course- like any serious anthropological researcher- I filmed him and shared it across social media. The German club and I made numerous jokes during the opening ceremony- like when the announcers only occasionally translated the speakers' speeches into English.

"You can tell they're not saying anything important," one person told me.

"Why is that?" I asked.

"Because even the announcers aren't translating it!" he replied in jest.

When the ceremony was finally over- and the flag bearers received their much needed bathroom breaks- the semi-finals for women's individual foil began. The two bouts pitted Inna Deriglazova of Russia against Arianna Errigo of Italy and Alice Volpi of Italy against Ysaora Thibus of France. Deriglazova would end up with the gold medal for the event, with Volpi receiving the silver and Thibus and Errigo receiving the bronze. (In individual events in fencing, the two athletes who lose in the semi-final round tie for third and do not fencing in a "bronze medal bout.")

Inna Deriglazova was born in Kurchatov, Russia in 1990 and began fencing at eight years old. She later went on to receive a law degree from Southwest State University in Kursk, Russia. But

Deriglazova's greatest accomplishments to date have definitely been through her fencing career. In 2010, Deriglazova earned the bronze medal in the European championships. In 2012, she earned the gold medal at the European championships and the silver medal in the team event at the London Olympics.

In 2013, Deriglazova earned the bronze at the World Championships in Budapest and later took the gold in 2015 at the World Championships in Moscow. The following year, Deriglazova took the gold medal at the Rio Olympics and in 2017 took the gold again (for three consecutive years) at the Leipzig World Championships after receiving the silver at the 2017 European Championships.[28]

Arianna Errigo was born in Italy in 1988 and began fencing at six years old. Like with most Italian fencers, Errigo as of 2017 was serving in the Italian Armed Forces- but her greatest accomplishments have come through her sport. Shortly before the Leipzig World Championships, Errigo earned the nickname "TsunAri (a play on words with the word tsunami) and for good reason. Between 2009 and 2017, Errigo earned three bronze medals and two gold medals at the European Championships; between 2005 and 2017, Errigo earned four bronze medals, three silver medals, and two gold medals at World Championships; and at the London Olympics in 2012, Errigo earned the silver medal.[29]

Alice Volpi was born in 1992 in Italy where she is currently a police officer. She began fencing in 2000 after her father suggested she try it out. Between 2009 and 2017, Volpi earned one bronze and two gold medals at the European Championships; between 2009 and 2017 earned one bronze, two silver, and one gold at World Championships; and as of 2017 has yet to compete at the Olympic level.[30]

Ysaora Thibus was born in Guadeloupe (a Caribbean island territory belonging to France) in 1991. There, she began fencing at seven years old before moving to France ten years later. Originally, Thibus wanted to be a ballerina, but after her mom brought little Ysaora and her brother to try a fencing class, Thibus quickly became addicted to stabbing other children with pointy swords and thus transitioned from princess to warrior princess. Between 2012 and 2017, Thibus earned two bronze medals at the European Championships; between 2009 and 2017 earned two bronze medals at World Championships; and competed in both the London and Rio Olympics finishing sixteenth and fifth places respectively.[31]

Historically, foil fencing is the longest existing women's fencing event at the Olympics, which means that there is a long list of historic foil fencers from the women's game. The top countries for producing female foilists have been Italy, Germany, Hungary, Russia, and Great Britain. These women include for Italy Irene Camber, Antonella Ragno-Lonzi, Maria Consolata Collino, Dorina Vaccaroni, Giovanna Trillini, Valentina Vezzali, Margherita Granbassi, Elisa di Francisca, and Arianna Errigo.

For Germany were Helene Mayer, Olga Oelkers, Heidi Schmid, Helga Mees, Cornelia Hanish, Zita-Eva Funkenhauser, Sabine Bau, Anja Fichtel, and Rita Koenig; for Hungary Erna

Bogen-Bogáti, Ilana Elek, Ildikó Újlaky, Ildikó Schwarczenberger, and Magda Maros; for Russia Valentina Rastvorova, Elena Novikova-Belova, Galiba Gorokhova, and Inna Deriglazova; and for Great Britain Gladys Davies, Muriel Freeman, Judy Guinness, and Gillian Sheen.

Elena Novikova-Belova of Russia is actually the only woman in the history of the Olympics to earn the Pierre de Coubertin medal for outstanding sportsmanship and the advancement of the International Olympic Games, so- obviously- I'm going to talk about her. Novikova-Belova was born in Sovetskaya Gavan, Russia in 1947. She was the first woman to earn four Olympic gold medals in fencing.

By the end of her Olympic career (which lasted from 1968 to 1980) earned a total of one bronze medal, one silver medal, and four gold medals. After the fall of the Soviet Union, Novikova-Belova moved to Belarus to advance women's fencing there and for her work in improving the quantity and quality of women's fencing in Belarus; Novikova-Belova earned the rarely awarded Pierre de Coubertin medal from the International Olympic Committee.[32]

While these countries dominated vertically (historically), a different set of nations dominated at foil fencing horizontally (contemporarily). Ahead of the World Championships, the top ten female foil fencers in the world were Lee Kiefer (USA), Arianna Errigo (Italy), Inna Derigazova (Russia), Ysaora Thibus (France), Nicole Ross (USA), Elisa di Francisca (Italy), Ines Boubakri (Tunisia), Hyunhee Nam (Korea), Astrid Guyart (France), and

Eleanor Harvey (Canada).[33] After wiping away the vertically excelling nations, this leaves the United States, France, Tunisia, Korea, and Canada as the emerging nations for women's foil fencing.

US and Canadian fencers typically train with each other- especially fencers in Toronto and New York City because of the close proximity. Tunisian women often go to France to train, so those two usually pair together like Canada and the US. Korea is a unique country for fencing however. [South] Korea relatively recently emerged into the sport of fencing and has been playing "catch-up" with the continent of Europe. These fencers have rapidly made a name for themselves in the sport as excellent fencers, but- due to the drive to raise the level of competition created in Europe over a hundred years- Korean fencing has a unique culture in the sport that ignores the European culture of the sport.

Few Korean fencers adhere to the unofficial rules of the sport, which define the American and German styles (like not kicking one's mask in anger). At one point during a men's bout, a Korean fencer was ignoring completely the Western manners of the sport when he went over to an angry opponent and coy-fully tapped his shoulder in joust- which in all honesty should have actually been a penalty. (While watching, my response was simply, "fuck that guy.")

Essentially, in the modernization of Korean fencing, the masters of the sport in Korea have ignored the long standing traditions of the sport defined largely by tradition and oral history in an attempt to rapidly climb to a level of international success which took countries like Italy and Russia a century to advance to. Thus, while fencers from France may train with fencers from the United States or those from Ukraine might train with those from Great Britain; fencers from Korea rarely train with fencers from outside their country.

"Vidlik" ONUKA

On 22 July, I left the hostel once more and headed for the arena to watch the women's individual saber. During the round of 32, Monica Aksamit of the United States was squaring off more against the referee than her opponent on the pisté. Even her coach was firing off on the referee over bad calls. In foil and saber fencing, when two fencers hit each other at the same time, only one person gets a point.

The referee determines who wins the point through a series of rules known as "right of way" much like how when two cars arrive at a roundabout at the same time determine who pulls into the circle first. In right of way for both saber and foil, the fencer who begins the attack first wins the point with the exception that if there is a successful parry from the second attacker, the second attacker receives the point.

This all sounds relatively simple, but a second statistic makes this incredibly more difficult. In the summer Olympics, there is only one piece of athletic equipment that moves faster than a fencer's sword- and it is the bullet leaving a gun. (Which means technically, a fencer's sword moves faster than an arrow leaving a bow.) When two saber fencers attack each other- it is usually done at the exact same time without any parries from either competitor, which leads the referee to make a "no-call" meaning neither person gets a point.

The referee during Aksamit's bout was making lots of no-calls and additionally made a lot of calls, which usually would award Aksamit the point- but instead went to her opponent. (In saber, an attack made with the sword while backing up- or retreating- is considered by most referees to not be an attack; as one cannot be on the attack and simultaneously running away. This referee thought differently.)

Aksamit and her coach were so infuriated at the referee's blatant ignorance at the common judgment for attacks that Aksamit received a red card penalty (in fencing this results in the fencer's opponent receiving a free point) due to her coach yelling at the referee. Aksamit lost the bout, saluted her opponent and shook her hand, then left the strip in tears of outrage. This is a good time to talk more about fencing tradition. In fencing, there are a set of unofficial rules and official rules, which govern an athlete's behavior.

Minor rule breaks result in "yellow card" penalties- which function as warnings for unintended fouls (for example, a body chord that does not function properly). Intentional rule breaks result in "red card" penalties- which function as positive punishment for intentional fouls (like yelling at the referee) and result in a point awarded to the opposing fencer. Then there are "black card" penalties- which are heinous fouls committed. This can include throwing one's mask, using foul language at an opponent or referee, or cheating; and results in the forced removal of the fencer from the tournament and can include other penalties like suspension for an extended period of time.

There are also unofficial rules in fencing known only to people who have trained with Maestros who's line of training with their own Maestros, etc goes back centuries. In the tradition of fencing, a fencer should never turn their back to their opponent (after a bout, a fencer should walk backwards from their opponent and maintain eye contact after shaking hands), should never speak directly to their opponent (addressing the referee if their opponent needs to tie her shoes or fix their equipment), and should never yell or shout during a bout.

This collection of unofficial rules continues on, but it all revolves around the nature of the sport of that of respect. Whether infantry, cavalry, or aristocratic civilians; fencers historically were in a sport where they were required through laws of respect to honor their opponent in combat. This aspect of the sport is changing though, but for the most part most Americans adhere to the unofficial rules of respect in the sport.

After Aksamit's bout, she maintained respect for her opponent through these rules and while she was certainly not happy at the referee- nor was her coach (nor was I actually for that matter)- she adhered to the unofficial rules of respect for her opponent after the bout. Soon after, I started watching the Sara Balzer bout, but after the first round, she took a bad injury to the leg and had to withdraw from the competition. All of the saber fencers I went to watch were knocked out through either injury or defeat, but sitting next to me was yet another fencing mom- this time from the UK.

She was watching the bouts with two fencers- one representing Great Britain (her daughter) and one representing India. The four of us talked about the expense of the sport and how many athletes have to choose between paying for the sport and having a job. Often in fencing the best fencer in the world will immediately stop competing not because of injury or because their athletic career has peaked, but because they can no longer afford to keep competing. That means the best swordswomen in the world are rarely ever actually at the Olympics or World Championships.

In the case of women's saber, the perfect example of one of these women in Rebecca Ward- known better as Becca Ward. In 2012 Ward was favored to win Olympic Gold at the London Games after her medal winning performance four years earlier in Beijing, but decided not to compete at all because she valued her education more and decided to graduate from college instead of taking a year off to train. Ward was at the time one of the greatest saber fencers in the world, but chose not to compete so that she could focus on school.[34] She later went on to never compete at the Olympics again opting instead to accept a job in ecological protection in Oregon.

The semi-finals for women's saber would see Azza Besbes of Tunisia square off against Irene Vecchi of Italy and Cecilia Berder of France square off against Olga Kharlan of Ukraine. Besbes and

Kharlan advanced into the finals with Kharlan finishing the tournament with the gold medal. Besbes earned the silver, and Berder and Vecchi earned the bronze medals.

Azza Besbes was born in Tunisia in 1990 and started fencing at ten years old. Besbes was born into a fencing dynasty including both her mother and her sister who are both major names in women's fencing- especially in their home nation of Tunisia. Both Azza and her sister moved to France early in their athletic careers because of the lack of financial support from their home country. Between 2007 and 2017, Besbes earned two silver medals and nine gold medals at the African Championships; between 2006 and 2017 won one bronze and one silver medal at World Championships; and competed in three Olympic Games in China, London, and Rio taking seventh, ninth, and sixth places respectively.[35]

Irene Vecchi was born in Italy in 1989 and began fencing at eight years old. Like with most Italian fencers, Vecchi is in public service as a police officer when not dominating at international competitions. Between 2007 and 2017, Vecchi won one bronze medal at the European Championships; between 2006 and 2017 won two bronze medals and one silver medal at World Championships; and competed at two Olympic Games in London and Rio finishing sixth and twenty-second respectively.[36]

Cecilia Berder was born in France in 1989 and began fencing in 1997. Berder now dual wields a sword in one hand as a fencer and a pen in the other as a journalist- meaning she probably laughs when people talk about which is more powerful. Berder aka "The Goat" originally wanted to become a mountain climber but settled for fencing because the rock climbing class was full that year. Berder has to date not earned any medals at any European Championships; but has between 2007 and 2017 earned one bronze and one silver at the World Championships; and finished in fifth place at her only to-date Olympics at Rio.[37]

Olga Kharlan was born in Ukraine in 1990 and began fencing at ten years old. Between 2007 and 2017, Kharlan won one bronze and five gold medals at the European Championships; between 2005 and 2017 won two bronze medals, two silver medals, and seven gold medals in World Championships; and competed in three Olympic Games in Beijing, London, and Rio earning the bronze in the latter two.[38]

Historically, saber fencing is the youngest women's fencing event at the Olympics, which means that there is not a long list of historic saber fencers from the women's event. The top countries for producing female saberists have been the United States, Ukraine, Russia, and China. These include for the United States Mariel Zagunis, Sada Jacobson, and Rebecca Ward; for Ukraine Olga Kharlan; for Russia Sofya Velikaya and Yana Egorian; and for China Tan Xue.

While these countries dominated vertically, roughly the same set of nations dominate at saber fencing horizontally. Ahead of the World Championships, the top ten female saber fencers in the world were Yana Egorian (Russia), Anna Marton (Hungary), Manon Brunet (France), Jiyeon Kim (Korea), Olga Kharlan (Ukraine),

Cecilia Berder (France), Mariel Zagunis (United States), Sofya Velikaya (Russia), Charlotte Lembach (France), and Irene Vecchi (Italy).[39] After wiping away the vertically excelling nations, this leaves Hungary, France, Korea, and Italy as the emerging nations for women's saber.

When I returned to the hostel at the end of the day, I stopped into the pub on the first floor. It was the first night I was having dinner there, so I asked the bartender at the bar to suggest a dinner. He told me I should get the wild boar schnitzel with house-made sauerkraut. After eating the massive feast, the bartender and I talked about Alaska. Another bartender occasionally stopped inside between cigarettes to join our conversation, and I impressed them by talking about brown bears and the Sitka Spruce (a species of tree endemic to Southeast Alaska) and how beer brewers use it to make specialty beers in the state.

"VANYA" Manizha

That night, I found new roommates in my hostel in the form of yet another fencing club from Germany. This group was three men about my age (25 plus or minus three years) who also came for the weekend to watch the tournament. While the Germans slept in, I woke up early and headed to the arena to catch the women's individual epee and found my roommates at the area shortly after my arrival. (Those bastards drove and made me take the bus like some kind of peasant.) The four of us sat down next to the Canadian women's epee fencers Leonora Mackinnon and Vanessa Lacas-

Warrick.

The two both started fencing in Canada at seven and eight years old and met with early success in the sport- which they both credit as their chief reason for staying in the sport. They opened up about the culture of fencing in Canada which functions more like Alaska than the continental United States. In the US, there are fencing clubs almost everywhere. With the exception of places like Idaho and maybe Maine, almost every state in the continental US has numerous clubs where a kid can enter the sport and find options for which "Maestro" to train under.

Competitions are mostly inter-club tournaments that pit anywhere from two to twenty clubs' fencers against each other. Alaska- where I teach fencing- is much different. With so few clubs (five officially registered with the national body), most club tournaments are only intra-club and most fencers who want to compete seriously must compete at either the national level (which Alaska has some serious competition by the way) or at the international level.

In Canada, it works about the same as in Alaska. There are few clubs- most centered in urban locations like Toronto and Vancouver- meaning fencers who want to compete regularly against people they do not train with must become national or international level competitors. (So, Vanessa and Leonora- if you're reading this- you are always welcome to come slay in Alaska at one of our five clubs! But Sitka's is the best.)

When the women's epee began, the two Canadian fencers

told me of the four bouts about to begin, that the [Sarra] Besbes v [Lauren] Rembi bout would be the one to watch because "both fencers have a unique style, but are equally good- so it will be interesting to see who comes out on top." At the competition, each bout of each round was usually going on at the same time- meaning during the round of sixteen, there were eight bouts happening at the same time. Thus, I had to focus only on about twelve percent of the total "action" unfolding in front of me- so unfortunately I had to make choices. Plus when the Canadians told me to watch one specific bout, I watched that bout.

During a pause in the bout, I turned to one of the fencers and asked her if she had an arch nemesis in fencing. (I had a whole family when I was competing who were my arch nemeses, so I was always curious if other fencers had enemies in the sport.) "I can't say I do," one answered. "But you know, there is a lot of drama in women's fencing."

"Really?" I asked.

"Yeah," she continued, but halted when the bout resumed.

When the bout ended, the team had dispersed and I was not able to learn about the secret rivalries in women's fencing. What I did piece together from an earlier conversation- with Jeff Spear's mom aka Mama Spear- was that there was a rivalry between one US foil fencer and a Canadian foil fencer. (I'm hiding names here because I would prefer that neither one of these world-ranked experts of swords do not show up at my house and stab me with pointy objects.) She did not remember how the rivalry began, but it did shed light on the "underground" drama of fencing which happens away from the pisté.

The semi-finals for women's epee would see Olena Kryvytska of Ukraine face off against Ewa Nelip of Poland and Tatiana Gudkova of Russia face off against Julia Beljajeva of Estonia. Unfortunately I did not get to watch these bouts with the Canadians. Nelip defeated Kryvystka and Gudkova defeated Beljajeva to reach the gold medal bout leaving the other two to earn the bronze medals. In the final bout, Gudkova defeated Nelip to earn the gold and Nelip finished with the silver medal.

Olena Kryvytska was born in Russia in 1987, but moved with her family to Ukraine after the fall of the Soviet Union. It was in her new hometown of Ternopil where she began fencing shortly after the move. As of 2017, Kryvystka has not yet won any medals at the European Championships between 2007 and 2017; has earned one bronze at World Championships between 2007 and 2017; and competed at two Olympic Games in London and Rio finishing thirty-first and fifteenth respectively.[40]

Ewa Nelip was born in Poland in 1989 and began fencing in fifth grade while in elementary school after seeing a recruitment poster at a local shop. Her fencing brought her all the way to the United States where she fenced at Notre Dame (a powerhouse in women's fencing in the US) and even briefly worked as an NCAA coach for the collegiate team. Between 2008 and 2017, Nelip had not yet placed in any European Championships; between 2005 and 2017 earned two silver medals at World Championships; and has yet to compete at any Olympic Games.[41]

Tatiana Gudkova was born in Russia in 1993 and began fencing in 2002 after finding dissatisfaction in basketball, dancing, and gymnastics. Between 2010 and 2017, Gudkova earned one bronze and one silver medal at the European Championships; between 2011 and 2017, she earned three gold medals at World Championships; and has- as of 2017- not yet competed at any Olympic Games.[42]

Julia Beljajeva was born in Estonia in 1992 and began fencing ten years later when her aunt invited her to try the sport. Between 2009 and 2017, Beljajeva earned one bronze at the European Championships; between 2008 and 2017, she earned one bronze and one gold at World Championships; and competed at the Rio Olympics finishing at twenty-ninth place.[43]

Historically, epee is the "middle child" of women's fencing at the Olympics, which means that there is a not a long list of historic epee fencers from the women's event. The top countries for producing female epeeists have been France, Hungary, and China. These include for France Laura Flessel-Colovic, Valérie Barlois-Mevel-Leroux, and Maureen Nisima; for Hungary Gyoengyi Szalay-Horváth, Tímea Nagy, Ildikó Mincza-Nébald, and Emese Szász-Kovacs; and for China Sun Yujie and Sun Yiwen.

While these countries dominated vertically, a different set of nations dominated at epee fencing horizontally. Ahead of the World Championships, the top ten female epee fencers in the world were Sarra Besbes (Tunisia), Emese Szász-Kovacs (Hungary), Sun Yiwen

(China), Rossella Fiamingo (Italy), Tatiana Logunova (Russia), Injeong Kim (Korea), Irina Embrich (Estonia), Kong Man Wai Vivian (Hong Kong), Julia Beljajeva (Estonia), and Nathalie Moellhausen (Brazil).[44] After wiping away the vertically excelling nations, this leaves the Tunisia, Italy, Russia, Korea, Estonia, Hong Kong, and Brazil as the emerging nations for women's epee.

That night, I decided to head back to the hostel's first floor pub and talked with the bartenders again who- after my discussion of women in fencing- were beginning to pay attention to the news around the event. While talking to the bartenders, a man sitting nearby joined in before introducing himself as a Zen monk. He and I talked about what led me to becoming a researcher of women's sports (and the very zen-like path that led me into it) as well as the different experiences of women and men in corresponding careers (including sport and religion). Since he was enjoying the conversation, the priest bought me more beers to keep me talking- and I never say no to free alcohol- so I stuck around until I was on the verge of falling asleep from both the time and the beer.

"One, Two Step (feat. Missy Elliott)" Ciara, Missy Elliott

The women's individual epee was the last individual event for the tournament, which signaled the beginning of the team events. Team fencing events carry with them a combination of controversy and politics. At the Olympic level, team fencing events reached "full capacity" in that all three men's and all three women's events were in the games by 2004 when women's saber was added to the roster.

Since then, the International Olympic Committee thought it was a good idea to only allow four total team events out of six each Olympic Games- meaning one men's event and one women's event was cut from the games for that round of four year. Typically, the World Championships permit the Olympic Games to count as that year's championships; but to maintain each event's world championship bouts; the FIE has to host it's own World Championships each Olympic year for only two events.

What all this means is that since 2004, there are waves of elite athletes who get "snubbed" from competing at the Olympics because of the IOC's "bright idea." Luckily, the IOC decided this "bright idea" was not so bright after all and announced shortly before the 2017 Fencing World Championships that all six team events would be back at the Olympics for the 2020 Games in Tokyo.

At the Rio Olympics, the two events denied from the games were men's saber and women's foil. These were also the first two-team events to play out at the Leipzig World Championships. When I arrived at the arena on 24 July, I sat down next to the general manager for Team USA to watch the USA men's saber team square off against Georgia. We talked about how she ended up as the general manager (originally a manager for Team USA field hockey, then switched jobs when the position was available), about Sabrina Massialas' recovery from the previous injury (and about Nzingha Prescod's arrival as her alternate), and about the bout itself playing out before us.

When the bout was over, I headed over to go watch the

women's team foil bouts and inadvertently ended up sitting behind Team USA athletes Race Imboden and Miles Chamley-Watson. These are certainly two interesting characters in the narrative of fencing's history. Typically, it is rare that people can actually name historic fencers- since for such a long time it has been considered an amateur sport. In fact, most fencers themselves cite coaches and instructors as their role models rather than fellow athletes. That should make these two more impressive then, when I write that when I asked all the youth volunteers who their favorite fencers were- these two were the most common answers.

Now, admittedly, I did not fangirl over these two as much as the twelve year-old girls at the tournament did; but I did notice a sort of stoic heroism in them. Apart from being the top fencers in the United States, being among the top fencers in the world, and- strangely enough- being runway models- there was one moment involving these two, which earned my high respect. Before the women's foil bouts started, one of the men from the French team sat down next to these two to hang out. There was one team USA fencer (I'll hide the name here), who walked by on her way to go practice in the warm-up area.

As she walked past, the French fencer remarked, "Oh nice, there's [insert name here]."

"Yeah," Chamley-Watson replied, "She's a beast."

The Frenchman continued, "She's so [beautiful]."

The two American fencers then immediately went into a conversation about the fencer's badass fencing records to shut that

French fencer down- trying to explain her worth as a fencer instead of her worth as a sex symbol. As the two corrected their friend, I found myself nodding in respect from two rows behind. (And if either or both of you two are reading, well done guys.) With that, the USA vs China bout began. During the bout, Margaret Lu (USA) took a pretty nasty injury to the ankle- another injury at the tournament. When Nzingha Prescod came into the bout, the competition was pretty much over and the US won.

After a brief lunch outside the arena, I returned to watch the next round of bouts, which included a bout between Italy and Germany that began with a sort of war dance from the Italian women. Since the tournament was being held in Germany itself, the German fans were in full force cheering and whistling as the team battled Italy for the chance to enter the semi-finals.

In team events in fencing- two fencers (one from one team and one from the other) compete against each other, then switch to the next pair- like a batting order in baseball (but if there were only pitchers and batters and nobody else). In the team event there are nine total rounds, and the highest score possible is forty-five points. If one team reaches forty-five points before the end of nine rounds, that team wins; and if the time runs out in the ninth round, whichever team has the highest score wins.

This becomes a bit more complicated at the round level. The first two competitors can only reach a maximum of five points before the next round of fencers. Imagine for a moment the pole vault competition where at the end of each round, the bar is brought to a greater height. The first round starts with a five-point limit for the team score, and that number increases by five each round. For example, the highest score possible a team can have at the end of round seven is thirty-five points- this means each team bout must enter nine rounds.

This becomes yet more complicated when discussing individual score limits. Each individual fencer has a ten point score limit per round- so if during the seventh round, one team starts with thirty points and another starts with fifteen; once the second team reaches twenty-five points- even if the first team only has thirty-two or if there is still time on the clock- the round ends. This prevents any team from relying on only one great athlete.

The "batting order" also staggers meaning two opponents never face off against each other twice- much like the way pool bouts work where each fencer competes against each opposing fencer exactly once. Each team has a three-fencer batting order with a fourth person designated the "anchor" or substitute- typically brought in for either round eight or round nine and whose task is to finish the bout as the least exhausted teammate.

In the semi-finals, Team USA squared off against Team Russia; and I somehow managed to find myself as the only Team USA fan surrounded by Russia's cheering section. During the USA v Russia bout, Lee Kiefer sustained an injury- making her the third of five total USA women's foil fencers to take an injury at the tournament- but after some quick spray-can pain killer returned to the bout. USA went on to win the bout against Russia, which included the wounded Lee Kiefer ending the bout hopping about and screaming the way I imagine the mythological sprites might sound like as she hopped her way into the arms of her victorious teammates and into the finals.

Italy defeated Germany in the semi-finals, so while the US and Italian teams took a break before their final competition; Germany and Russia faced off for the bronze medal. In team competitions, there are no shared bronzes, so the two defeated semi-finalists must fence in a bronze medal bout. As well as the bronze medal bout, other defeated teams must also continue to compete to determine official fifth to sixteenth placements- meaning that if a team loses once, they have to keep fencing.

During one of these bouts, a member of the Canadian team had to pull out of the tournament due to an injury to her arm- adding to the list of battle-wounded in Leipzig. By the end of the day Italy managed to come out on top to earn the gold medal against the United States in the finals, and Russia defeated Germany to earn the bronze. Team bouts in fencing can be unique in a number of ways- but largely because it forces a nation to field at least four elite-level athletes.

This means that nations like Tunisia, which might supply one, or two individual women's foil fencers in a tournament may not be able to supply a team for the team event. That makes team events a great example of historic nations dominant in a given weapon. The nations represented at the women's team foil event at Leipzig were (in order of final standings) Italy, USA, Russia, Germany, France,

Canada, China, Japan, Hungary, Poland, Korea, Hong Kong, Sweden, and Argentina.[45]

"Papercut (Kor.)" OOHYO

The following day, I continued along on that early morning grind by waking up and heading over to the arena for the second day of the team events- this time including men's epee and women's saber. In the rounds of 8, Team USA fell short in both events to emotional defeats. As the audience shuffled over to the main seating areas to watch the semi-finals, I stayed behind to observe the defeated Americans as they wiped away their sweat and prepared for the long day of "placement bouts" to determine just where on the list the American flag would wind up.

During the next wave of bouts, the American women squared off against Russia. During the bout, Monica Aksamit (USA) sustained a pretty nasty injury requiring the medical staff at the venue to intervene. While receiving medical aid, Aksamit also received a visitor in the form of her opponent- Yana Egorian (Russia)- coming by to check up on her competitor (in a much more friendly manner than the previously discussed Korean athlete). At the end of the bout, Russia came out on top.

After a team bout, each fencer shakes hands with each of their opponents- like in soccer or volleyball- then with opposing coaches, then with referees; then finally they must sign a paper listing the final scores. After the American women signed away the last step of the post-bout ritual, they took to the cubical sideline by the pisté and mulled over their defeat. The athletes and coaches met this moment first with silent reflection, then with tending to their phones to check in on social media.

Next, they collected their masks and swords, and unzipped their uniforms to let the stifled hot air escape. Once the literal and figurative hot air had time to escape, the athletes and their coaches rejoined and quietly discussed the chain of events that led to their defeat and prepared for the next round of bouts that would determine their placement in the final record books.

The semi-finals for women's team saber would see Italy face off against France and Korea face off against Japan. The Italian women seemed animated- prepared for their opportunity to enter the finals. The French responded to their animated opponents with silent stoicism as they prepared mentally rather than physically for the bout ahead. Throughout the bout, the French remained silent on the sidelines as one among them in turn battled the Italians favored to win.

By the seventh round, the French team however engulfed themselves in fiery passion as athletes and coaches alike urged on their combatants on the strip. At one point in the seventh round, there was a moment of such incredible athleticism, that at the end of it- the two opposing athletes responsible immediately high-fived each other in amazement. (And, yes; of course I'm going to describe this badass moment.)

First I want to pre-empt this play-by-play to talk about scoring in saber bouts though. Usually, each play lasts about one third of a second (and this is not an exaggeration) because as soon as the referee starts the clock; both fencers thrust themselves forward from only about ten feet away, their swords hit each other, the clock stops, and the referee makes a call. (This is why there is no time limit in saber.) With that being said, the fact that the event I am about to discuss even happened at all is worthy of serious standing ovations. (Which it received.)

As the referee started the clock, the French fencer thrust herself against the Italian, but the Italian (instead of thrusting her own self forward) parried the attack, then reposted (a counter-attack); but failed to hit her retreating opponent with the repost. But don't believe for a second things ended there. The Italian charged forward- taking the offense and roaring forward on the strip with continuously violent sword-work. With one foot outside the back line, the French fencer halted her retreat and thrust back with a parry against the Italian's attack and a lunge forward with her repost. It landed. France gets a point. The two athletes high-fived. Somewhere in the afterlife, Anne Bonny cheered in approval.

Eventually, Italy managed to win the bout and advanced the final. Korea defeated Japan as well- sending Italy and Korea into the finals. France would go on to defeat Japan in the bronze medal bout to earn a third place finish and Italy would defeat Korea in the final to earn the gold medal. The team saber competition included almost twice as many teams as the foil event, and the final placement tells an interesting story of the history of women's saber. The final placement ended with (in order) Italy, Korea, France, Japan, Russia,

Ukraine, USA, Mexico, Hungary, Poland, Spain, Hong Kong, Belarus, China, Canada, Germany, Azerbaijan, Kazakhstan, Venezuela, Turkey, Thailand, Georgia, and Dominican Republic.[46]

The list- almost like a proverbial totem pole among the Indigenous Peoples of Western North America- tells a history of women's saber that at the top mostly stand the nations who have produced Olympic-level saber medal winners since the event joined the games in 2004, while the lower nations on the list are countries where both saber fencing- and fencing overall- are growing and may within the next two to three Summer Olympics could be producing medal-winning saber fencers.

"591" Enno Cheng

On the last day of the Leipzig World Championships, the venue would play witness to the final two team events- men's foil and women's epee. As the men competed at the arena, the women warmed up and prepared for their final shot at bringing home medals for their respective nations. By this time, most of the athletes who were competing at the tournament had already packed their backs and left. There were few audience members left- since it was no longer the weekend, and people had to go to work- which left few people at the arena to cheer on the athletes. I was not about that at all, so on the final day- I cheered more than I ever had before.

When the round of 16 began for women's epee, I sat down to watch the United States take on Italy. The American women who made up the 2017 epee team were Kat Holmes, Kelley and Courtney Hurley, and Anna Van Brummen- and in that specific order is a sociological litmus test of (from first to last) intimidation to gleefulness. If Anne Bonny (the famous pirate I refer to endlessly in this ethnography) had somehow reincarnated in the form of a contemporary fencer- it would be Kat Holmes.

As she warmed up heading into the bout- my immediate thought was that somebody is going to be stabbed- a lot- and it's going to hurt- a lot. Then there's Anna Van Brummen who- much like Lee Kiefer during her spritely prancing about victory dance- is the kind of person who will not only congratulate her opponents at the end of a bout, but will probably also bake everyone a tray of peanut butter cookies so that everyone can be friends after stabbing each other painfully.

Now, I have to admit here (and Team USA women's epee, please don't pillage Sitka over this), I was not expecting the US to win. Italy's women's epee team has one of the top ten women's epee fencers in the world (Rossella Fiamingo) and as of April 2017, the US had zero.[47] When the Italians performed their ritualistic war dance to intimidate the US team, I prepared for the worst.

I was pleasantly surprised however. Van Brummen held the team afloat with her cheerleading, C Hurley swash-buckled her way across the scoreboard, K Hurley battled her way against stiff competition, and Holmes essentially terrorized the Italians into submission with her war face. By the end of the bout, the United States had won. Italy- this time- would be the team performing the post-defeat ritual.

After a round of men's bouts, the quarterfinals for the women's epee began and would see the United States square off against China. Again, China had one fencer in the top ten rankings (Sun Yiwen) with none from the States. The US had however upset the Italians, so I knew- even if the US lost- they would still make a strong name for themselves in this bout. When I sat down to watch the bout, a young mother and her two infant children sat next to me in the stand to watch the United States. After the initial introductions and questions of "Where are you from/ where are *you* from..." the bout began.

"I'm trying to introduce my children to sports," the mom spoke during a pause in the bout.

"And you're starting with fencing?" I asked- puzzled at the idea that fencing would be someone's first sport. (Even in Germany, everyone starts with soccer.)

"Neither one of them really like soccer," (There it is.) she replied. Her three year-old son wiggled around in his chair. "I don't think he likes fencing as much as his sister," she responded. Her daughter- about the same age- had eyes wide open while watching the American women. "She loves the US women," the mom continued. "They're her favorite."

I started talking about each US fencer in the bout- about Kat Holmes' intimidating gaze, about the Hurley sisters and how they remind me of the long-gone Nadi brothers, and of Van Brummen's impeccable sportsmanship. (I better get some peanut butter cookies for that, Anna!) This was not the only time I spoke with a mother-and-daughter pair of audience members at the tournament. Once before, I spoke briefly with a mom and her teenage daughter who had recently started the sport. I remember the daughter explaining how much she loved the sport after only being involved in it for about three years.

The interesting thing about fencing tournaments at the national or international level is that there is a wealth of people with vastly different levels of experience that show up. Some are men and women who have long retired from the sport and are now either simply fans or have taken managerial roles (like coaching staff). These represent the fencers reborn into new roles in the sport. There are the athletes themselves- whether competing or watching- who are at the center of the life cycle of fencing. Finally, there are those just starting the sport that do not yet know where it will take them or how long they will remain as athletes. These are of course the novices aka the n00bs, and it is this group that I believe is the life of the sport.

With coaches (maestros), this group is the proverbial silver-backed gorillas tasked with leading their clubs or teams, imparting their wisdom learned through decades in the sport, and passing on the oral history of fencing. The Olympians represent the role models of the sport. These athletes represent the image that young fencers strive to become- the Achilles, Ajax, and Penthisilea whose names history will remember (even if only in the oral accounts).

At the heart of fencing, the sport is made up of the unnamed men and women and boys and girls who- with unbroken swords and untested armor- are putting on a mask for the first time. These are the little girls going to see their heroes at the World Championships or shake in nervousness when they find themselves asking Yana Egorian to sign a t-shirt they just bought.

After considering all of this, it should be impressive then; that this little three year old girl from Germany who barely spoke English looked on with wide open eyes to watch her favorite fencers- the US women's epee team- compete in a bout. While China defeated the US in an emotionally ending game, the US women achieved something much more important in defeat than China did not achieve in victory- they put on one hell of a show for that little girl who is probably going to become a seriously badass fencer one day- and will have four American women to thank for it.

When the family sitting beside me left to watch other bouts, I stayed behind to support the US team through the rest of their day's bouts. They would have to keep competing after their heartbreaking loss for final placement in a bout against Russia. The United States managed to win the bout and finished with an overall placement of seventh as the last American women competing at the tournament.

China went on to earn the silver, losing to Estonia in the gold medal bout. Poland and Korea squared off for third place with Poland coming out on top. By the end of the day, the final standings were (in order) Estonia, China, Poland, Korea, Germany, France, USA, Russia, Italy, Ukraine, Israel, Hong Kong, Hungary, Spain, Romania, Argentina, Japan, Canada, Kazakhstan, Sweden,

Venezuela, Finland, Singapore, and Costa Rica.[48]

Over the next two nights, I mulled over my experiences at the tournament by sifting through photos I took as well as photos athletes at the tournament began posting on social media. There was one photo I took that stood out in my digital photo album among what was probably over two hundred images. In the picture, the US women's epee team stood shoulder to shoulder in a phalanx-like formation as the Italian team performed their war dance. The American women in the image look unimpressed ahead of what would be one of the most impressive feats of athletics I've seen in the sport. The image encapsulates the very nature of the sport.

Without prize money or fame, the only gain earned in investment as an athlete in the sport is friendship. There was an infographic I saw online somewhere that talked about how pirates spend their whole lives looking for buried treasure when the real treasure is the friendship those pirates make along the way. In a laughable sort of way, that's the sport of fencing.

Those fencers who focus solely on winning medals (ahem, Korea) miss out on the most important aspect of the sport- making friends in countries no one's ever heard of; having stories few people can comprehend, and living more in a split second than most people do in a decade. The stress of trying to win, the anger at loss, the high of victory, and the companionship of a team that endures all of those emotions together- even if sometimes they have to compete against each other- are what fencing is all about.

So after thinking about all of that, my obvious next action

was to get shit-faced hammered to wash away all those hippy emotions. (No you're crying!) I spent the evening with a man from South Africa as we drank various potent potables in the hostel's kitchen before heading down to the bar. This all of course began after I had already had a couple beers in the afternoon before a nap- so when I wandered back into the bar, the German woman who worked there was surprised to see me.

"You're back!" she replied excitedly.

"I know," I returned with despair. "I was just going to have a beer at five, but now these guys convinced me to come down here. Do you have coffee?"

"Oh," she returned, "We just turned off the machine for the night."

"I've been drinking all day," I broke down, "And they just keep giving me more alcohol and I never say no to free alcohol, and now I'm here and I hoped there would be coffee…" I rambled on for what was probably a depressingly long amount of time.

The woman became sympathetic to my plight though when she responded, "I could make some Turkish coffee!" [Made when grounds are boiled directly in the water and served without filtering the grounds out of the water.]

"Really?" I replied with wide, tearful eyes.

"But it might be pretty foul," she continued.

My face became reminiscent of a lost puppy that finally found its owner. "Thank you," I spoke with tears forming." Five minutes later, the woman reappeared with coffee to my gratitude and

I drank the brew while the other guys drank theirs. That coffee could have awakened the dead- and was exactly what I needed. I survived the night without even having a hangover (and if you're wondering, I gave that woman a ten Euro tip).

Chapter 3: Retreat

"Life" Zivert

After recovering from a long two nights of drinking my emotions away, I left Leipzig and headed south (on the correct train this time, I might add!) toward Munich. While I began my own post-tournament vacation, most of the fencers who competed at the tournament began their own. Ines Boubakri (Tunisia) posted videos of her and her mom visiting New York City. Kat Holmes posted an image of ice cream and beer on instagram (the breakfast of champions?) and Monica Aksamit posted images and videos of her trip across Italy.

After arriving in Germering (the small town outside of Munich which housed my hostel), I found myself in the trunk of a questionable blue van en route to the destination. I imagined it would be the ideal place for rest and relaxation after two weeks of intense anthropological observations because the hostel was also a restaurant and brewery; so I figured I would get some high quality Bavarian food and drink before heading home to Alaska.

It was not exactly what I imagined in my head. That night, I found myself at a hostel of mostly American guests managed by New Zealanders/Macedonians who didn't speak German, and found that the "brewery" was really a small bar supplied by a nearby brewery with a somehow unlimited tap. (And before you start thinking that last part sounds amazing, I will tell you now- sir or madam- it wasn't!)

Evidently every American teenager with a signed permission slip from their dad (this was somehow a thing) was staying at this hostel during my stay. I spent three nights watching high school and college-age Americans drinking beer out of shoes, peeing and puking all over hostel dorms, and being the most sober person at the place (because the staff were just as drunk as the guests). But God damn it if those weren't some of the best nights of my life.

I remember the diversity of the group of people we were with distinctly. There were potheads, meth-heads, hotel employees, college freshmen, physicists, athletes, Trump supporters, and Jill Stein voters. There was really nothing all of us could agree on, and there were a lot of times at least one among us felt very out of place. During a trip to the nearby lake for a midday swim, a young Canadian woman in the group decided to stay out of the water because she felt out of place with the noon-drinkers.

I refrained from drinking beer from a shoe because I felt out of place with people drinking alcohol out of shoes- even when they decided to be classy by drinking *wine* out of a shoe. (To each his/her own.) But at the end of everyday, every one of us came together over food and beer- and never the gourmet Bavarian pork chops, but cheap pizza and bbq- and found a way to get along despite all of our vast differences.

Plus, being the most sober guy at the place- even though I was far from sober- made me the guardian angel of the group. When the boys too young to grow mustaches beyond two hairs got too drunk to stand; I was the guy who showed up with a bucket and a glass of water- mostly because that guy would be sleeping in my room later that night, and I had no intention of playing "the floor is bodily fluids." The entire atmosphere was addictive for the lot of us.

Two among us (a Brit and an Australian) had come to the hostel a month before for a weekend stay and never left. A couple from California had extended their stay for three more nights after their initial two. Perhaps it was the shoe-beers (aka shoe-ies), but something about this hostel was dragging people inside and keeping them from leaving. When my planned three days at the hostel were over, I left early in the morning and headed for the train station.

"Ca me vexe" Mademoiselle K.

My train headed back to (almost) where my journey began. With less than four nights left in Europe, I decided to head back to Genoa, Italy to the castle of a hostel to enjoy my last nights in Europe. After another strenuous climb up a hot, steep mountain of a hill to reach the hostel. I checked in, took a cold shower, and went down to the kitchen area to meet some of the new guests at the place. (Unfortunately, all of the former guests who had been there when I left had all gone.)

I met an anthropological-minded couple from Montana who were in Italy starting a trip that would take them across Europe like I had been a month prior. During our conversation, a woman from Australia who was also studying anthropology joined in. The four of us didn't have long to talk though since we were running close to curfew for the hostel. After speaking for about an hour about my trip and about our lives in Montana and Alaska (similar states) and about Australia (not like Alaska or Montana), the staff kicked us out and we all headed to our respective rooms and went to sleep.

At breakfast, we reconvened over breakfast cereal and coffee and continued our conversation from the previous night. After the couple from Montana checked out and left for their next destination, the Australian woman (we'll call Sydney) and I went on a grocery run and stocked up on some overly sized bottles of wine before heading to the beach. While there, we waded into the waters below Genoa and talked about the differences between various zodiacs around the world (Greek, Chinese, and Mayan).

We talked about the eclectically large realm of American Anthropology (which for non-anthropologists reading this includes archaeology, biological studies, linguistics, and sociology). After our trip to the beach, we grabbed pizza and went to town on our wine bottles, which we shared with a group of three German men while we played several card games with them over dinner.

The card games went well into the night- sending us to a balcony of the castle overlooking the city where we played "Werewolf." In Werewolf, players attempt to guess who a designated werewolf is who is terrorizing an in-game town at night by attempting to guess which "villager" (player) is the werewolf. After playing several rounds of the game, our group dispersed for bed.

The next day, Sydney and I got lunch at the pizza place (the marathon continues) and hung out at the hostel before she too eventually checked out and headed to her next destination on her own trip across Europe. Along with my second phase of vacation, other fencers from the tournament began posting videos and pictures from their post tournament trips including Sarra Besbes (Tunisia) who got married, Nathalie Moellhausen (Brazil) who attended said wedding, and Courtney Hurley who took a road trip with her dogs from Montana to New Mexico. (By the way, Courtney Hurley's dogs win the "cutest dogs on instagram" award.)

All of these athletes well deserved their long awaited vacation time. Between (and including) the Rio Olympics and the Leipzig World Championships, there were seventy-eight women's fencing tournaments for those women who competed at Leipzig over the course of twelve months. That means if a fencer was from a country that could field a team for team events she would have competed in twenty-six fencing tournaments in twelve months. (And that does not even include tournaments at university or national levels, satellite events, or open events.)

Later that night, I had dinner again with the Germans (if you guessed pizza, you're correct) before turning in for an early bedtime. While trying to fall asleep that night, I looked over the results from the season's international tournaments to look for patterns that might help decipher what nations historically not known for women's fencing would become the next region of the world to dominate in the sport by the time the Olympics reach Los Angeles in 2028.

In the epee individual event, the ten most common countries

to medal were Estonia, Russia, Poland, Hungary, Italy, China, France, Korea, and Ukraine. This means the most common nations to win medals in the individual women's epee event were from Eastern Europe- with outliers in East Asia and the Western Mediterranean. This could mean that in the future, nations like Spain and Japan could become powerhouses in the event by the LA Olympics.

For the women's individual foil, there were only seven total countries that ever had fencers make the semi-finals in all individual women's foil events; which means that these seven nations have this event on lock down with stiff resistance against new nations becoming champions in foil. These seven nations were Italy, Russia, the United States, France, Tunisia, Korea, and Germany with two of those countries far from the European epicenter- the United States and Korea. (While Tunisia is certainly not in Europe, I have included it in the European sphere of influence due the nature of Tunisian women training mostly or completely in France.) That all means that at the Los Angeles Olympics, these are the most likely nations to provide medal-winning women foilists.

For saber, only ten nations ever supplied medal-winning fencers at the international level during the season. These were France, Italy, Russia, Hungary, Korea, Ukraine, Japan, Romania, the United States, and Tunisia. Saber- because it is still such a young event for the women's game- is still hard to say which nations will become the powerhouses within the next ten years.

The United States started in 2004 as the monopoly on

women's saber, but with more competition spreading as other nations with historical ties to the sport played catch-up in the last ten years; the United States largely lost their advanced lead. Now, nations like Japan and Korea are advancing quickly to rise to admirably victorious levels. In the Los Angeles Games, any of these nations hold a high probability of placing on the podium for women's saber. In the morning, I packed my bags, checked out of my room, charged my electronics, headed for the train station, and awaited the last train that would carry me through Europe. This final voyage would bring me back to Milan where I would eventually have to board a plane and say goodbye to a summer trip that took me far beyond my own expectations.

I only spent one night in Milan and I had done such a good job at conserving my money during the trip, that I decided to treat myself to staying at an actual hotel (do people my age use these anymore?), which had the coolest indoor pool. After taking a brief nap after check-in, I spent two hours soaking up some chlorine in the pool and met several families on vacation in Italy. After taking a shower to wash the "public pool" smell out of me, I headed to the hotel restaurant for an actual gourmet meal of the best lasagna I've ever had in my life.

The next morning- actually at 3:30am- I headed down to the lobby to check out and found out that my flight was leaving from an airport one hour drive outside of Milan and that there were no public transport buses running that early in the morning to get there. I ended up having to pay a hundred Euros for a cab, but managed to get to the airport two hours before my flight. That's when I saw the line for check-in at the airport.

In the United States airport check-in lines have nifty little walking tarmacs separated with that belt-buckle looking rope to guide people through organized lines and prevent chaos. Evidently, Italy has never heard of that because everyone was in one giant crowd. I lifted by luggage bag over my head like Donkey Kong and rampaged through the crowd to a check-in desk- only to find I was at the wrong one and had to cross the human swamp of frequent fliers once again- only to find out *there* that I had to go somewhere else to print by boarding pass first.

Thirty minutes later, I spent eighty total Euros printing a boarding pass and checking one luggage bag before I finally got into the line (another chaotic mob) for security. But I didn't have to take my shoes off, so that was nice. I then spent the next twelve hours on flights back to the United States, and did not get an upgrade to first class; which means I had to just sit there like some peasant without unlimited movies and having to pay for food. (And by the way, what airline does not provide free coffee to customers? This is outrageous.)

The first flight took me from Milan to Cologne where I would have to get on a second plane and head to Seattle. After accidentally passing the baggage claim, I headed out of the terminal through exit security and immediately started looking around for where I was supposed to find my duffel bag. After asking the information desk as to just where the baggage claim was supposed to be, I learned that I was supposed to get my bag *before* leaving the terminal.

For international readers, this is entirely strange in the United States. In the US, baggage claim is always outside the security checkpoints. Luckily, a very friendly German security guard walked me back into the terminal and helped me find my bag and find where my next flight's terminal would be. (Much better than Italy's system for sure.) When she looked at my passport, the security guard asked where I was from.

"I was born in Missouri, but I live in Alaska," I answered.

"Alaska!" she responded excitedly. "I've always wanted to go there!"

The officer brought me to the baggage area and helped me find my bag before leading me out of the terminal. When I finally got into the right area of the airport, I headed to my gate and awaited my final flight back to the US. Along the way, I broke my brain trying to figure out the time difference between Germany and Alaska and eventually gave up after I lost all ability to think rationally from the jet lag that overcame me.

After the plebian flights, I finally landed in Seattle and made it through security in under an hour (which is miraculous for an international flight). I hopped on the light rail and headed into the city where I would be staying with a Couchsurfer host who had hosted me during my fiasco in Seattle the previous summer. "You bastard!" greeted my designated Seattle-based friend. "You're over here traveling all over Europe with beautiful women and posting everything on instagram while I have to sit here in Seattle all summer!"

Seattle and I hung out over the next couple days reminiscing about past adventures we had both been on and about future adventures yet to encounter. On 7 August however, it was time for me to finally head back to Sitka. I packed my bags and headed to the airport. Once there, I got through security without having to pay money for a boarding pass (seriously Italy, this is why your economy is so terrible) and headed to get lunch with two hours left before my flight was even scheduled to start boarding.

I sat down at a table in the crowded food court and welcomed a pair of travelers to join me when all other tables were taken. One was a band manager and the other a poet and both talked about the importance of finding both work and friends that they enjoy. They had both been on a stag excursion (men's retreat) to an island in Washington State and were all separately on their ways back home. After they left I headed to the record store, bought a new Sleater-Kinney album (#feminism), and headed for my last flight of the long and adventurous trip.

"When I See U" Fantasia

Upon arrival back in Sitka, I found myself asking once again; "How do I tell a story of a sport expressed in unwritten emotion?" Fencing is a sport in which women sacrifice everything- financially, physically, emotionally- for what a more business-minded person might describe as nothing. Perhaps fencing- not physics- is poetry.

It's the expression of rare emotion only released through the protective mask of the fencer. So how do I tell the story of this unfiltered emotion?

Well, I can tell that story by telling my own. As I mentioned far earlier in this book, anthropology is a rare career that can never be replaced with machines- at least not the version of anthropology American anthropologists practice. When Franz Boas went out into the wilds of northern Canada to live among the Inuit in his first journey outside of New York, he found value in learning about a group of people by learning how those people see themselves and the world around them. He forged friendships and returned to Columbia University to practice a new philosophy in American social studies- a philosophy of empathy-based field research.

More than a hundred years later, I found myself asking on the plane to Europe whether there is still a need for field research in anthropology- especially my field where athletes continuously post on social media and sporting event statistics are readily available online. But this trip showed me there is still a need for in-person ethnographies, not only because of the valuable resources (aka athletes' moms) I encountered along the way- which I never would have found online- but because of the stories untold in this book. There were moments where I watched the sun rise over the hills of Genoa, of train rides through the Austrian Alps, and of all the incredible friends I never knew I had that I met during this trip.

I remember Jeff Spear once asked me during my conversation with him and his mom what- in my opinion- was the difference between socio-cultural anthropology and journalism. I told him, "A journalist knows how to ask questions, but an anthropologist knows how to listen." An anthropologist has to read body language, understand the message told in silence, and above all else- to live in the moment and know when to put down the field journal and get up and dance.

There's an emotional art in anthropology that requires an anthropologist to live by a code of "seize the day" because there will come a day when- if by some means one among us actually manages to get a real job after years of bush-whacking through the Amazon Rainforest or kayaking the Yukon River- we have to put away our dozens of field journals onto a bookshelf to collect dust and accept that getting dental insurance is kind of important. Someday, maybe sooner than I'd like- I have to embrace that truth. One day I'll have to retire my war-torn backpack, stash away my worn-out passport, and look at the field journals on my bookshelf like old paintings hanging above a fireplace.

At some point every athlete in fencing must stand on their proverbial shore and ask where to go next- to keep trudging along in a sport that poisons their credit rating, which destroys their wallet, which risks financial ruin for no prize money and little recognition. That dilemma defines the experience of athletes in the sport of fencing. For what other sporting event ends with two bitter enemies shaking hands and giving high fives when something impressive results in their ruin; what other sport plays witness to banshee-like screams of victory and waterfall-proportioned tears in defeat; and what other sport ends with the best fencer in the world having to skip the Olympics because they need to pay rent?

I cannot speak for the women of fencing- as that would just be serious "mansplaining" on my part- but I can speak as an anthropologist who has walked the pisté (as the fencers would say) in their shoes. So to you reader, I say this. Get out there. Whatever it is in your life that causes the greatest outpour of emotion- whatever ends in your violent screeches from the depths of your soul in response to glorious victory or the tears unshed through months of unreleased sadness in response to utter defeat- get out there and do that thing. Play the trumpet if you must, as you quit your desk job and charge triumphantly towards your adventure into unemployment.

There is one fencer in the world I respect more than any other- and she is not my favorite fencer. (Nicole Ross, if you are reading this, I respect you infinitely, but there is one person I respect infinitely more- if that is mathematically possible.) This is a woman who I think perfectly encapsulates everything that I have written about in this ethnography- Monica Aksamit. I have spoken briefly about this fencer earlier in this book, but this is a fencer who deserves more than any other (and maybe this is only my opinion) to have her story told.

In 2016, Aksamit qualified as an alternate for the US Olympic saber team. Like most fencers in the world she struggled with finances, but persisted (Elizabeth Warren style) to make her way onto the team for the Rio Games. She then turned to crowdsourcing to raise fourteen thousand dollars to pay for her flights, lodging, and everything else she needed to pay for in order to compete as the anchor at the Summer Olympics in Brazil. Once there, she was part of a four-woman team that earned the bronze medal where she stood shoulder to shoulder with the greatest swordswomen in the world- including her teammates Mariel Zagunis (aka the Highlander), Ibtihaj Muhammad, and Dagmara Wozniak.

I never got to speak with Aksamit during the Leipzig games. There was one day though, when I was leaving the venue to go get lunch and I passed her on the sidewalk as she was heading inside. I smiled and she smiled back (and I fangirled really hard immediately after). Fencing is difficult for everybody. Women and men struggle just to have enough money to compete. And they cannot do it forever. I don't know how many more Olympic Games Monica Aksamit has left in her.

Perhaps she'll be the next Valentina Vezzali- or maybe Rio will be her only Olympic Games. But- if under the rare chance that the fencer I respect more than any other happens to be reading this- I have a message for you and for every woman in fencing still competing out there. Please, keep going; for as long as you can. There are young women and girls out there who see you- either in person at World Championships or on TV during the Olympics- and to them you are everything. For as long as you can, for those little girls out there, keep going.

"Next To Me" Emeli Sande

Two pirates once met on a ship en route towards a treasure hunt. The first of the two was the newly elected captain, young and new to the life of piracy in the waning Age of Sail. The other was old, seasoned by years on the sea and in battle. The old pirate came to the young captain with a limp leg and a slow stride brought on by old age and injury. "Are we on the right track?" asked the young captain.

"Aye," replied the elder.

"I'm curious," replied the captain, "just as to why you decided to board my ship."

The older pirate grinned and looked down to the aged wooden planks that formed the deck of the ship. "You refer to my age?" the pirate responded.

"Aye," replied the captain.

"You're young," spoke the elder. "There was a time I stood in your place. When I was a young captain leading my ship on its first treasure hunt- into the world against a sea of a thousand foes." The young captain smiled before returning to the horizon.

"I survived a hundred battles at sea," continued the older pirate. "I raided towns and forts and villas on beaches you have probably never heard of. I mastered the art of the sword and the pistol and danced in the moonlight with men of all walks of life." The pirate paused in sadness. "I survived," the old pirate continued. "When my carpenter died, and my boatswain passed on, and even the cook left the ranks; I found myself with a crew of men who had no idea who I was. So I left my ship and settled down. I found a nice home on an island overlooking the sea and started a family."

After a brief pause, the young captain worded, "And?"

"I began to see the water on the horizon the way you might see a painting hanging over a fireplace- some strange piece of art that you might walk past a hundred times and never notice. For fifty years, I never even set foot on another boat again."

"And now?" the captain asked.

"All of my family is now either dead or moved away," the elder continued. "In my old shack on the island, I heard a cry for adventure seekers wishing to find riches under a new pirate captain in town. For the first time since retirement, I smelled the salt in the ocean breeze once more. That is why I joined your crew, Captain."

"That's quite the story," the young pirate replied.

The elder of the two turned to meet the younger with an expression of advice. "You're young," the elder spoke. "Take this from someone who has stood in your place before." A pause. "Keep going. From all of us who gave it up and forgot the smell of the sea, keep going. For as long as you can. Because one day- if god forbid you survive the battles and the raids, and the dancing in the moonlight- one day you will forget the smell of the sea and it is the worst tragedy that can befall someone that stands where you stand."

Epilogue

"Kids Only" Leah Dou

For Seventeenth Century women, piracy represented an escape from oppressive patriarchal norms. Even in the Twenty-first Century, the idea that a woman would leave the life chosen for her to pursue a life of sword fighting (or any sport) continues to baffle patriarchal societies to the point that most female athletes across sport cultures struggle to afford a lifestyle extravagantly funded for male counterparts. For women in fencing, the financial mortality of life in the sport prevents some of the best athletes in the world from reaching their full potential.

After the Leipzig World Championships, most of the women who competed began planning for their last Olympics that would see either their final moment of triumph or last stand in the Tokyo Games in 2020. Unless some organization finally starts paying the women of fencing to pursue their sport- allowing them to finally pay rent on time- fencing's chief problem will continue to be plagued by the inevitable truth that the best fencers in the world are not competing at the Olympic Games.

Perhaps- once again- I am the most qualified person to have conducted this ethnography. After finishing the field research on fencing, I almost immediately departed for the next trip. I traveled to California and Hawaii to document the lives of women in surfing and after several pineapple smoothies and shrimp tacos; my bank account began demanding my resignation. After taking a handful of boring jobs to pay the rent and spending almost the last of my savings to make sure the utilities office didn't shut my water off, I began planning what will probably be my last ethnography.

Like with fencing, anthropologists are almost never paid- usually only through book sales (which can get expensive when advertising is almost exclusively through book tours). But over my four years of documenting the lives of women in sports- like with women in fencing- I gained a currency immeasurable in paper money. I laughed my way through the Women's World Cup in Canada with people from New Zealand, France, and England.

I hitchhiked my way through the American West with people who served in the Air Force, taught piano, and bred horses. In Europe, I sat on beaches with people who taught me how to use Snapchat, had a picnic in Switzerland with people who worked on the Large Hadron Collider, and ate bbq in Germany with people who drank from shoes. Finally- in California and Hawaii, I danced in the moonlight with men and women from all walks of life. (Read all about it in *Behind the Break*!)

Like with the women of fencing, I earned a currency of emotion- something I don't think anyone can ever earn sitting behind a desk. But with a bank account depleting rapidly and the smell of the sea fading- and with my passport getting seriously torn up from sand, heat, and water- eventually I will need to give it all up. And the worst part of all of this is that the two pirates from the story *were* men.

"Always with You" Aseul

If this were a high school essay in Early World Literature class, Mr. Reidelberg would want me to answer the final question- "What is a hero?" If women in fencing are heroes, they would need to have answered at least one of the four universal questions. Where did we come from? Why are we here? What does it all mean? Where do we go when we die? Many athletes in sport retire from their athletic career and take to writing- with several athletes writing memoirs detailing their entrance into their sport and a few writing about the history of their sport. There are several books that detail the history of women in rodeo, connecting the lineage of cattle herding in the early American West to the development of the sport, and the establishment of the Women's Professional Rodeo Association.

Then of course there are women in soccer who write about the role of both individual athletes and the obstacles they fought to overcome in making the sport more inclusive for future women. There are even dozens of anthropologists who grapple with the symbolism of surfing and women's roles as environmental protectors and the relationship between being and place among the waves. But perhaps fencing- the sport of both the future and past, blending ancient weaponry with electronic technology- is the sport, which attempts to question what happens when it all ends.

I remember from my university fencing club's guest seminar with Nicole Ross who spoke about quitting her day job to train for the Olympics. She reminded us (and probably herself) that when her athletic career ends, she could always return to a desk job- but the opportunity to be an Olympic fencer would not exist forever. While certainly death only in the metaphorical, fencers always keep that final question in the back of their minds- where do I go when my fencing career dies? They certainly won't have any money for early retirement (in fact they are probably too behind on social security that they'll never be able to retire).

In Italy, Valentina Vezzali- arguably the greatest fencer of all time (regardless of gender) became a politician in the Italian Parliament.[49] In France, Laura Flessel became the National Minister of Sport.[50] In the United States, Becca Ward went on to work in legislative assistance with a focus on environmental protection.[51] Eventually, each athlete that survives the years of sword fighting scars, international flight costs, and expensive meals in foreign countries walks away from their life in the sport, finds a quiet corner of the world, and starts a new life. So, here at the end of this whole ethnography- what is a hero, Mr. Reidelberger?

In the novel *Siddhartha* by Hermann Hesse, the main character goes from being the son of a wealthy merchant to engaging in a journey to question his faith, experience love, explore the world, and- ultimately- find himself among the ever flowing river of time and space. A hero is not defined by the charismatic speeches bellowed before battle, for enemies slain, or unseen wonders discovered. To be a hero is simply defined and rarely achieved. To question one's place in their world, to explore new ideas and

lifestyles, to experience love, and to answer the universal questions-
these are what make a hero. After several months of research and
several weeks of my own journey- I've come to learn that women in
fencing have each earned that title.

Like with the pirate queens of the Age of Sail, women like
Monica Aksamit, Nathalie Moellhausen, and even Freya Clarke saw
an opportunity to choose a new path towards adventure that
challenged the lives their societies may have chosen for them. And
none among them are likely wealthy enough to become the best they
could be, but in the end- these three women are all heroes not for
writing memoirs, their medal counts, or for advancing their careers
beyond imagining. They're heroes because they keep going for as
long as they can; and every once in a while, when their knees hurt
and they sit down in the bleachers and contemplate retiring from the
sport, a little girl comes to them and asks for a signature- and the
new generation of women in fencing begins.

"Yellow Flicker Beat" Lorde

In 2020, Olympic hopefuls planning on competing in the
Tokyo Olympics were told they would have to wait another year. A
dangerous influenza outbreak known as COVID-19 (because it broke
out in 2019) rapidly spread across the planet and forced several
sports leagues to shut down their seasons early and postpone several
sporting events- including the Summer Olympics.

At the time, the vast majority of those women athletes hoping
to compete in the Olympics that year had already put their money

making lives on pause to prepare full-time for the tournament. While all agreed they would prefer not dying because of the outbreak, several athletes were frustrated that they would have to endure more time not making money to recompense years of a sports career that makes almost no money.

Two and a half years after conducting this study, it's hard for me to predict the future of women's fencing- or fencing at all for that matter. The technology, infrastructure, and leadership all exist to keep the sport running; but for the vast majority of athletes competing in it, there is just not enough money to keep them competing. Italy's unbalanced medal count shows just how important pay is in sports. The athletes who have jobs that accommodate their competition (like the police or military) have the necessary funding and time for competition.

Even in the case of sponsored athletes, the sponsorship money doesn't amount to much. When I first spoke with Nicole Ross back in 2014 about coming out to visit my collegiate fencing club, she told me her partnerships could essentially pay for the flight and hotel- but that's about it. Fencers with sponsorships usually still do not make enough money to pay their rent, phone bills, or groceries without side jobs. A similar problem faced major league baseball way back during the time of Babe Ruth. The guy had a side job at a factory before he left Boston because the Red Sox couldn't pay him a livable wage.

The difference here however is that fencing just doesn't bring in big enough crowds or revenue to have the league pay their athletes- men or women- livable wages. That means unlike baseball, fencing will probably soon see and end to its Golden Age- the age of individuals pouring their hearts out into a sport that represented a dying niche where women could dare risk their lives to be something they chose for themselves rather than society.

As more countries embrace Italy's model of employing Olympians in their police and military; those athletes become not only socially acceptable, but state-sponsored. This could seem as a win for these athletes, but the problem becomes when an athlete is sponsored by a government with questionable human rights records. Russia is one of the countries that often employs Olympians in its police and military. (Imagine being a woman athlete sponsored by a government that puts women in prison for making punk music videos.)

You can almost think of these athletes as privateers- the pirates who have state-sponsored piracy. Just as the mass employment of privateers brought about the slow decline of piracy in the Caribbean, so too will this model bring a major shift in the culture of international fencing. Without pay, there is only so far fencers can reach in their sport; but without the independence to be who they decide to be for themselves, there is only so far these athletes can reach in life.

Fencing Playlist

"No Instructions." KATIE. LOG. Axis; 2019.
"Rupture." Laurie Darmon. Mesure premiere. Mercury Music Group; 2015.
"Conqueror." AURORA. All My Demons Greeting Me As A Friend (Delux Edition). Glassnote Entertainment Group; 2016.
"So Gone." Monica. After The Storm. J Records; 2003.
"Comportement." Aya Nakamura. Journal intime. Warner Music France; 2017.
"Giovani fluo." Asia Ghergo. Giovani fluo. Asia Ghergo; 2017.
"Si vedono i fiori." Flora. Si vedono i fiori. Flora; 2019.
"Christine." Christine and the Queens. Chaleur Humaine. Because Music; 2014.
"Planes, Trains, Automobiles." Julia Wu. 5 am. ChynaHouse Digital; 2019.
"Non non non (Ecouter Barbara)." Camelia Jordana. Camelia Jordana. Sony Music Entertainment; 2010.
"Le canzoni fanno male." Marianne Mirage. La canzoni fanno male. Sugar; 2017.
"Vidlik." ONUKA. VIDLIK. VIDLIK; 2016.
"VANYA." Manizha. VANYA. Manizha Sanghin; 2019.
"One, Two Step (feat. Missy Elliott)." Ciara, Missy Elliott. Goodies. LaFace Records; 2004.
"Papercut (Kor.)." OOHYO. Papercut. Mun Hwa In; 2018.
"591." Enno Cheng. 給天王星. Fire On Music; 2019.
"Life." Zivert. Life. Первое Музыкальное Издательство; 2019.
"Ca me vexe." Mademoiselle K. Ca me vexe. Roy Music; 2006.
"When I See U." Fantasia. Fantasia. 19 Recordings; 2006.
"Next To Me." Emeli Sande. Our Version of Events (Special Edition). Virgin Records; 2012.
"Kids Only." Leah Dou. Kids Only. Grey Waters; 2017.
"Always with You." Aseul. Always with You. Astro Kidz; 2018.
"Yellow Flicker Beat." Lorde. Yellow Flicker Beat (From The Hunger Games: Mockingjay Part 1). Republic Records; 2014.

Works Cited

Andrews, Evan. "5 Notorious Female Pirates." History Stories. A&E Television; 23 June 2015.

"Beljajeva Julia." Fencers. FIE; 2017. Web. 10 July 2017.

"Berder Cecilia." Fencers. FIE; 2017. Web. 9 July 2017.

"Besbes Azza." Fencers. FIE; 2017. Web. 9 July 2017.

Boissoneault, Lorraine. "The Swashbuckling History of Women Pirates." Smithsonian Magazine. The Smithsonian Institute; 12 April 2017.

"Coups de Monde; Cancun." Results. FIE; 14 October 2016. Web. 2016.

"Coups de Monde; St. Maur." Results. FIE; 4 November 2016. Web. 2016.

"Deriglazova Inna." Fencers. FIE; 2017. Web. 9 July 2017.

Ebrey, Patricia. "Women in Traditional China." Center for Global Education. Asia Society; 2018.

"Errigo Arianna." Fencers. FIE; 2017. Web. 9 July 2017.

"Grand Prix; Turin." Results. FIE; 2 December 2016. Web. 2016.

Goe, Ken. "Olympic fencer Rebecca War will be inducted into the USA Fencing Hall of Fame." The Oregonian; 19 June 2014.

"Gudkova Tatiana." Fencers. FIE; 2017. Web. 10 July 2017.

Hussain, Leila and Knight, Matthew. "Valentina Vezzali: Olympic fencer turned political jouster." CNN; 22 April 2015.

"Kharlan Olga." Fencers. FIE; 2017. Web. 9 July 2017.

"Kryvytska Olena." Fencers. FIE; 2017. Web. 10 July 2017.

"London Isn't Calling." Duke Magazine. Duke University; 3 June 2012. Web. 9 July 2017.

Murphy, Michaela. "Was There a Gender Revolution in the Seventeenth Century?" Brighton Arts. University of Brighton; 16 November 2012.

"Nelip Ewa." Fencers. FIE; 2017. Web. 10 July 2017.

"Paris 2024 congratulates Laura Flessel-Colovic on her appointment as Minister of Sport for France." Association Internationale de la Presse Sportive; 18 May 2017.

Prescod, Nzingha. "What It's Like to Be a Black Female Olympic Fencer." Marie Claire Magazine; 26 July 2016. Web. 8 July 2017.

Puchko, Kristy. "9 Female Pirates You Should Know About." Mental Floss; 19 September 2014.

Studeman, Kristin Tice. "Olympic Fencer Monica Aksamit is Ready to Slay at Rio 2016." W Magazine; 27 July 2016. Web. 8 July 2017.

"Thibus Ysaora." Fencers. FIE; 2017. Web. 9 July 2017.

"Valentina Vezzali." Sports-Reference.com; nd. Web. 8 July 2017.

"Vecchi Irene." Fencers. FIE; 2017. Web. 9 July 2017.

"Volpi Alice." Fencers. FIE; 2017. Web. 9 July 2017.

Wilson, Joseph. "Anthropology of Fencing; Interviews with Emma Baratta and Eva Jellison." Email correspondence; 2016.

Wilson, Joseph. "Anthropology of Fencing; Interviews with Manon Brunet and Martina Criscio." Email correspondence; 2017.

"Women and Islam." Oxford Islamic Studies. Oxford University; 2018.

"Women's Epee individual- Fencing; Atlanta 1996 Summer Olympics." Olympic Database; nd. Web. 25 July 2017.

"Women's Foil individual- Fencing; Paris 1924 Summer Olympics." Olympian Database; nd. Web. 25 July 2017.

"Women's Individual Epee." Results and Statistics. FIE; 2017. Web. 21 April 2017.

"Women's Individual Foil." Results and Statistics. FIE; 2017. Web. 21 April 2017.

"Women's Individual Saber." Results and Statistics. FIE; 2017. Web. 21 April 2017.

"Women's Team Epee; World Championships." Results: List of Results. FIE; 2017. Web. 12 July 2017.

"Women's Team Foil; World Championships." Results: List of Results. FIE; 2017. Web. 11 July 2017.

"Women's Team Saber; World Championships." Results: List of Results. FIE; 2017. Web. 11 July 2017.

"Women's Sabre individual- Fencing; Athens 2004 Summer Olympics." Olympic Database; nd. Web. 25 July 2017.

Whitman, Walt. "O Me! O Life" Leaves of Grass (1892). The Poetry Foundation; nd. Web. 24 July 2017.

"Yelena Novikova-Belova." SR/Olympic Sports. Sports Reference; 2017. Web. 10 July 2017.